THE SATYRICON

Also by Martin Foreman

Novels
Weekend
The Butterfly's Wing

Short Stories
A Sense of Loss
First and Fiftieth

Plays
Angel
Californian Lives
Casanova Dreaming
Now We Are Pope
Tadzio Speaks (*aka* Death on the Lido)
Ben Jonson's Volpone

Non-Fiction
AIDS and Men (ed)

martinforeman.com

THE SATYRICON

a play

Martin Foreman

adapted from the text
by Gaius Petronius

Arbery Books

arberybooks.co.uk

January 2023

Published by Arbery Books
17/5 Craigend Park, Edinburgh EH16 5XX
printed by copyshop.co.uk, Redditch B98 8LG

ISBN: 978-0-9933546-6-3

Acknowledgements

Many thanks to Junior Cross, without whose encouragement and involvement in the early stages of rehearsal this play would not exist.

Thanks also to the actors who participated in the workshops that would have led to a 2020 production if Covid had not intervened, to the cast and crew of the 2022 run and to the Edinburgh Graduates Theatre Group for their support for that production.

Thanks as always to my partner Somdee Dechchai, who continues to tolerate and forgive my many eccentricities in our life together.

Martin Foreman

for current and past productions of the play see

thesatyricon.uk
and social media
@thesatyricon / @thesatyriconplay

Cast

The Satyricon was first presented at the Assembly Roxy Theatre, Edinburgh, on 5 October 2022 with the following cast:

CHARACTERS

Gaius Petronius	Stephen Corrall
Encolpius	Joseph Cathal
Ascyltos	Ben Blow
Giton	Scott Adair
Trimalchio, Bacchus	Alastair Lawless
Eumolpus, Old Woman	Robert Wylie

ACTORS

Agamemnon, Priapus, Ship's Mate etc	Trev Lord
Quartilla etc	Wendy McEwan
Daphne, Circe etc	Rhona O'Donnell
Doris etc	Karolina Oleskiewicz
Innkeeper etc	Kelly Louise Edie
Lichas, Steward, Constable etc	Lachlan Robertson
Fortunata, Tryphaena etc	Lois Williams

Notes

This script is based on the original production with some lines omitted and others added or amended. Lines within [ ] are specific to that production (such as in Scene 7 when the Mate tells Doris he looks like Agamemnon) and need not be retained. Occasional directions are given only to clarify the text and can be ignored. The script and casting may be adapted as follows:

CHARACTERS

Encolpius, Ascyltos and Giton must not be doubled with any other part.

Petronius can be doubled with Trimalchio with minor changes to the text in Scene 9.

The role of Bacchus is optional.

The roles of Eumolpus and the Old Woman can be allocated to the Actors.

ACTORS

All roles (Agamemnon, Quartilla etc) can be allocated to any Actor. Priapus is optional. Cross-gender casting is acceptable but pronouns cannot be changed.

LINES AND SCENES

The text is not inviolate and can be adapted to local circumstances. Minor changes such as replacing Scottish / British phrasing and vocabulary are allowed without consultation. Changes that involve cutting lines, changing humour, plot or attitudes (for example to imply approval or disapproval of behaviours) and changes that cut or shorten a scene require the author's permission in advance of rehearsals.

ACT ONE
SCENE 1: THE AUDITORIUM

[BACCHUS laughs]

PETRONIUS	Ladies and gentlemen, welcome to...
ACTOR	Pssst!
PETRONIUS	Ladies and gentlemen,
ACTOR	Pssst!!!
PETRONIUS	Excuse me. What is it?
ACTOR	You've forgotten . . . *(inaudible)*
PETRONIUS	Must I?
ACTOR	If you don't, I'll walk.
PETRONIUS	All right.
	Ladies, gentlemen and non-binary people, welcome to The Satyricon!
	My name is Gaius Petronius. I am an Arbiter - a judge - of elegance. Equivalent to, say, editor of *Vogue* - a commander in the Fashion Police.
	Strictly speaking, I *was* an arbiter. I've been dead for two thousand years. But my story . . .
ENCOLPIUS	Hold on, it's my story. I'm the one that tells it. It's all about me and what happens to me.
PETRONIUS	A minor point. I created you and I'm the one who put the words into your mouth.
ENCOLPIUS	It's still my story. I want credit.
PETRONIUS	And credit you shall get. Lights!

This, ladies, gentlemen - and non-binary people - is Encolpius.

Encolpius claims to have been a gladiator

ENCOLPIUS   What do you mean "claims"?

PETRONIUS   Throw him a trident and he'd stab his own foot with it.

ENCOLPIUS   That only happened once!

PETRONIUS   Let's be generous and call him a student, young, brash and with his eye on the main chance - although the main chance seldom has its eye on him.

ENCOLPIUS   We'll see.

PETRONIUS   Thank you, Encolpius.

Next up is Ascyltos.

ASCYLTOS   At your service.

PETRONIUS   Ascyltos should be the gladiator.

ASCYLTOS   Fucking right.

PETRONIUS   If there's a fight, he'll be in the middle of it, and if there's a fight he probably started it.

ASCYLTOS   Who, me?

PETRONIUS   He says he's a student. He can't remember what he studies but he maintains the age-old tradition of getting drunk regularly. And If he ever does reach old age he'll proudly tell you he's a graduate of the University of Life.

ASCYLTOS   That it?

PETRONIUS   That'll do for now.

Finally, there's Giton.

GITON   What am I supposed to do?

PETRONIUS   Strike a pose or take a bow.

                 What can I tell you about Giton? Well, he's
                 sixteen years old and just discovered sex.
                 What's the expression? Young, dumb and full
                 of cum. That's all you need to know.

GITON   Sixteen? I'm not sixteen. I'm [AGE OF ACTOR]

PETRONIUS   The character is sixteen! Good grief! How
                 many times have we gone through this in
                 rehearsal? What I was saying about dumb?
                 Typecasting. Go away.

                 I'd like to call them heroes, but they're not
                 handsome or virtuous and if they've got brains
                 they haven't yet learnt how to use them.

ENCOLPIUS   Thanks a bunch.

PETRONIUS   No matter, let's set them off on their
                 adventures and hope they get through them
                 unscathed. So, on with the Show.

                 Ladies , gentlemen and non-binaries, welcome
                 to...

ACTOR   What about us?

PETRONIUS   What about...? I forgot. Lights!

                 That lot are Actors. We'll bring them on when
                 we need them for minor roles. Until then
                 forget them.

ACTOR   Minor roles?!

ACTOR   Forget us? Thank you!

ACTOR   Fuck that!

PETRONIUS   I say they're Actors, but that's giving them the benefit of the doubt. They're only here because we couldn't afford anyone better. We pay peanuts, you get monkeys. They'll all play several characters, so pay attention and don't get confused when they turn up as different people in different scenes.

ACTOR   For fuck's sake, get on with it!

PETRONIUS   Indeed. Places, everyone.

               Ladies, gentlemen, non-binaries, The Satyricon!

SCENE 2: THE FORUM

PETR'IUS (cont) What are you waiting for?

BYSTANDER You haven't set the scene.

PETRONIUS I'm sorry. Our trio have just arrived in town. Encolpius has found his way to the Forum and, convinced as always that he has something important to say and people want to hear it, is haranguing the crowd.

ENCOLPIUS My friends!

BYSTANDER Who are you calling a friend?

ENCOLPIUS Friends!

Romans!!

Countrymen!!!

BYSTANDER Mind your language!

ENCOLPIUS I said "countrymen".

BYSTANDER Oh, carry on.

ENCOLPIUS Countrymen, lend me your ears!

BYSTANDER What's wrong with yours?

ENCOLPIUS My friends, what use is education today?

All students know is how to pass exams.

In the old days Sophocles and Euripides dealt with real issues affecting people's lives. Now, teachers offer only platitudes and cliches.

Plain-speaking Attic style is forgotten. Everthing is Asiatic - all flourishes, superficial.

BYSTANDER	I like Asian food. Mind you, it can be a bit spicy.
ENCOLPIUS	It won't last.
BYSTANDER	What? Asian food? You're right. Half an hour after a bowl of rice I'm hungry again.
ENCOLPIUS	Modern style. It'll be forgotten in a generation.
BYSTANDER	I've forgotten it already.
ENCOLPIUS	It's the teachers' fault. Anything for a quiet life. Doing it the easy way got them where they are today so why not pass it on?
AGAMEMNON	Young man, nothing could be further from the truth. Stand aside.
ENCOLPIUS	Do you mind?
AGAMEMNON	Not at all.
BYSTANDER	Here's another one.
BYSTANDER	He's better-looking.
BYSTANDER	Only if you're blind.
AGAMEMNON	It's not the teachers' fault, it's the parents'.
	Parents push their offspring too soon, too hard. No sooner is little Julius born than Mater and Pater are pushing him to succeed in public life so they can bask in his glory. They don't understand that patience, dedication and hard work are essential for a serious grounding in life and education.
BYSTANDER	Very true.
AGAMEMNON	Thank you.

BYSTANDER   What's your name?

AGAMEMNON   My name? It's . . . My name is . . . My name? Help me out here!

PETRONIUS   Agamemnon!

AGAMEMNON   Agamemnon, father of Electra, her of the Electra Complex who wanted to kill her mother and marry her father, that Agamemnon?

BYSTANDER   The King of Mycenae who reluctantly led the Greek forces against Troy?

BYSTANDER   His wife Clytemnestra was sister to the Helen who eloped to Troy with Paris?

BYSTANDER   The Helen whose face launched a thousand ships?

AGAMEMNON   The Agamemnon who returned from Troy to find his wife ...

BYSTANDER   ... the said Clytemnestra ...

BYSTANDER   ... had taken Aegisthus for a lover and was then killed?

BYSTANDER   Who was Aegisthus?

BYSTANDER   Who was killed?

ENCOLPIUS   Agamemnon was killed by Clytemnestra.

BYSTANDER   ... his wife ...

BYSTANDER   ... or Aegisthus ...

BYSTANDER   ... his wife's lover.

ALL   Is he that Agamemnon?

PETRONIUS   No! That Agamemnon had been dead for

hundreds of years. Of course he couldn't have been in the Forum. I wrote about another Agamemnon, a sophist.

BYSTANDER   A what?

BYSTANDER   He makes sofas?

AGAMEMNON   Why on earth did you choose that name?

PETRONIUS   Oh, never mind. Get on with it.

AGAMEMNON   As I was saying, Young people have no stamina these days.

BYSTANDER   You don't know my husband.

AGAMEMNON   We should all be concerned. The future of Rome is at stake.

BYSTANDER   Who cares, as long as there are bread and circuses?

AGAMEMNON   So serious is the situation that I have thrown off a poem that every youth, every adult, every statesman that sees the the danger to our nation should memorise.

Ahem...

If you would an artist be,

or, Heaven help us, politician,

accept advice I give for free

to help reach your ambition.

ALL   The word you need is discipline.

No drink and no frivolity.

Avoid the stage and ev'ry sin,

and leaders of the polity.

Let your guide be Socrates,

the wisest man who ever lived.

Harken to Demosthenes,

Use words as swords; be combative!

Drink deep the lines of Homer's verse,

Take as your model Cicero,

Lest you create terse verse much worse

Than that created long ago.

AGAMEMNON   Thank you! Thank you!

A-ga-mem-non. Two As, two Ms, two Ns.

No, only one E.

ENCOLPIUS   Hang on, where's Giton?

AGAMEMNON   Who?

ENCOLPIUS   My boy; he was here a moment ago. And Ascyltos?

AGAMEMNON   I have no idea.

ENCOLPIUS   I have to find them.

Whatever it takes, wherever they are, no matter how lost they may be or how much time I spend, or whatever sacrifice I make, I must find them.

AGAMEMNON   It is your duty.

ENCOLPIUS   It is my task.

AGAMEMNON   Your burden.

ENCOLPIUS   My quest.

AGAMEMNON   Your obligation.

ENCOLPIUS   Commitment.

AGAMEMNON   Commission.

ENCOLPIUS   Pledge.

AGAMEMNON   It is your Odyssey!

ENCOLPIUS   My Odyssey! My own adventure.

AGAMEMNON   And you are the hero!

ENCOLPIUS   The hero . . .

AGAMEMNON   Fare well, fair Ulysses.

ENCOLPIUS   Encolpius. Fare well, dark . . .

AGAMEMNON   Agamemnon.

ENCOLPIUS   Agamemnon. But not the Agamemnon, father of Electra . . .

AGAMEMNON   No, not that Agamemnon. Until we meet again.

SCENE 3: A STREET THEN A BROTHEL

ENCOLPIUS   Now, was it that way I came? Or that way? We came out, turned left, then right - or was it second right? Giton was hungry and he was looking for . . .

OLD WOMAN   You all right, dearie?

ENCOLPIUS   No, I'm lost.

OLD WOMAN   Where do you want to be?

ENCOLPIUS   Back at my lodgings. You don't know where they are, do you?

OLD WOMAN   Me? We've only just met, dearie.

ENCOLPIUS   It's a tall building. Lots of children running around outside. Landlady name of Drusilla.

OLD WOMAN   Drusilla? I know her. Tall, pretty, blonde, figure like a goddess?

ENCOLPIUS   No, she's short, fat, dark and got two hairy moles on her face.

OLD WOMAN   That's the one. Lovely girl.

ENCOLPIUS   She's as old as you are.

OLD WOMAN   That's what I mean, a lovely girl. You come with me, dearie. She's not far.

ENCOLPIUS   She must be. It took me an hour to get here.

OLD WOMAN   You must have come the long way, dearie.

ENCOLPIUS   I came straight down that road.

OLD WOMAN   Like I said. You must have followed the sewer, it winds all over the place. You always know where you are by the stink. Wind's in the west again.

ENCOLPIUS   Are you sure you know her?

OLD WOMAN   Who?

ENCOLPIUS   Drusilla!

OLD WOMAN   Of course, I do, dearie. You come with me, I'll take you to her. What's your name?

ENCOLPIUS   Encolpius. What's yours?

OLD WOMAN   Drusilla.

ENCOLPIUS   That's my landlady's name.

OLD WOMAN   So it is, what a coincidence.

ENCOLPIUS   Where are you taking me?

OLD WOMAN   I told you, back to your place.

ENCOLPIUS   This doesn't look like it.

OLD WOMAN   It's a short cut. In you go.

ENCOLPIUS   This isn't the entrance.

OLD WOMAN   We're round the back. Some people prefer the back passage.

ENCOLPIUS   Are you sure?

OLD WOMAN   Of course I'm sure. I've lived here all my life. You can trust me. I'm as honest as the day I was born. The ides of March, if I remember.

ENCOLPIUS   Well . . . I don't recognise this place.

OLD WOMAN   It's a bit dark here. Some of them like it like that.

ENCOLPIUS   Some of who?

OLD WOMAN	Clients.
ENCOLPIUS	Ow!
OLD WOMAN	Sorry, don't know my own strength. Just being friendly.
ENCOLPIUS	What are you doing? Get off!
OLD WOMAN	Thought you might like to thank me.
ENCOLPIUS	Thank you? For what?
OLD WOMAN	Bringing you home.
ENCOLPIUS	This isn't home.

They are surrounded by prostitutes and clients of various sexes and ages, including one in pursuit of ASCYLTOS

OLD WOMAN	I'll get you there. Just a little business first.
ENCOLPIUS	What business?
OLD WOMAN	This business.
ENCOLPIUS	I'm not interested.
OLD WOMAN	That's what they all say, dearie. Just give me time to get down to it and you'll be in ecstasy.
ENCOLPIUS	I'd rather be in my lodgings.
OLD WOMAN	Just a couple of sesterces. It's worth it, I promise.

ASCYLTOS and ENCOLPIUS bump into each other and fight off the encroaching crowd which scatters

.

SCENE 4: A STREET

ENCOLPIUS   Where the fuck were you?

ASCYLTOS   Around.

ENCOLPIUS   Leaving me lost in a strange town.

ASCYLTOS   You found some company.

ENCOLPIUS   So did you.

ASCYLTOS   I didn't fancy yours.

ENCOLPIUS   Yours wasn't much better.

               We've got to find Giton.

ASCYLTOS   He'll turn up. He always does when he's
               hungry.

ENCOLPIUS   I don't know where he puts it.

ASCYLTOS   I know where it comes out.

ENCOLPIUS   I hope you don't. That's my affair, not yours.

ASCYLTOS   Whatever.

ENCOLPIUS   We've got to find him. Handsome boy lost in
               the city. Anything might happen to him.

ASCYLTOS   Like it almost happened to you.

ENCOLPIUS   I can look after myself. He can't.

ASCYLTOS   Don't be so sure.

ENCOLPIUS   We need to split up. You go one way, I'll go
               another. We'll meet up back up at the lodging.

ASCYLTOS   Right you are.

ENCOLPIUS   Hold it!

ASCYLTOS	What?
ENCOLPIUS	Where is the lodging?
ASCYLTOS	The sign of the Cooked Goose. Next to the barracks.
ENCOLPIUS	Right.
	The Cooked Goose. I hope that isn't a bad sign.
	Giton!
	Where were you?
GITON	Where were you? You left me.
ENCOLPIUS	No, I didn't. One minute you were beside me, the next you were in that bakery. I went in, couldn't find you.
GITON	The baker's wife wanted to show me her baps in the back room.
ENCOLPIUS	What were they like?
GITON	Firm, thick and round, but I couldn't get my hands on them. She said I had to pay first.
ENCOLPIUS	Some women are like that.
GITON	I didn't have any money.
ENCOLPIUS	If I gave it you, you'd spend it.
GITON	So I stole them.
ENCOLPIUS	Saved one for me?
GITON	I was hungry.
	I missed you. Where were you?
ENCOLPIUS	In the Forum

GITON	Giving another speech? Doesn't sound like you missed me.
ENCOLPIUS	I did. I was coming home to look for you.
GITON	Took your time about it.
ENCOLPIUS	I got delayed.
GITON	By what?
ENCOLPIUS	An old woman.
GITON	What did she want?
ENCOLPIUS	You don't want to know. Then I met Ascyltos.
GITON	Oh, yeah. Ascyltos.
ENCOLPIUS	What does that mean?
GITON	Nothing.
	He tried . . .
ENCOLPIUS	He tried what?
GITON	You know. Called me Lucretia. I'm not a girl.
ENCOLPIUS	Thank the gods.
	Did you let him?
GITON	No! But he kept trying.
ENCOLPIUS	Didn't you tell him to stop?
GITON	I did, but he didn't.
ENCOLPIUS	So?
GITON	I said you'd beat him up.
ENCOLPIUS	That stopped him.
GITON	He burst out laughing. I told him I didn't want to.

ENCOLPIUS	Did he stop then?
GITON	More or less.
ENCOLPIUS	Did he?
GITON	Yes!
ENCOLPIUS	Sure you didn't want to?
GITON	Yes, I don't! Didn't! Whatever.
ENCOLPIUS	He's not bad-looking.
GITON	I know, but, you and me . . . And he's rough, not like you.
ENCOLPIUS	If it happens again, let me know.
	Shall we go?
GITON	Where?
ENCOLPIUS	Back home. It's this way.
GITON	No, it isn't, it's this way.
ENCOLPIUS	Are you sure?
GITON	That's the soldiers' trumpet. Bedtime.
ENCOLPIUS	Any time's bedtime with you.

SCENE 5:THE COOKED GOOSE

ASCYLTOS   Morning, Castor and Pollux. I see you finally got out of the sack.

ENCOLPIUS   I've a bone to pick with you.

ASCYLTOS   Chicken or duck? All I've got is stale bread.

ENCOLPIUS   Don't be funny. Giton told me what you've been up to. No wonder you didn't come back last night.

ASCYLTOS   I fell in with a couple of gladiators who'd got their freedom. The stories they told. The plans they had. Move to Sicily, get into the slave trade. Trouble is, they spent all their prize money on drink. Most of it. Some of it fell in my tunic. I mean, our need's as great as theirs.

ENCOLPIUS   Stop changing the subject. You tried to have it off with Giton. Don't deny it.

ASCYLTOS   I didn't say anything.

ENCOLPIUS   He told me everything.

ASCYLTOS   Did he?

ENCOLPIUS   Didn't you?

GITON   Yes, I did.

ENCOLPIUS   But you didn't, did you?

GITON   Didn't what?

ENCOLPIUS   Do it. You didn't do it.

ASCYLTOS   We didn't do it, did we?

GITON   No!

ENCOLPIUS   Are you sure?

GITON   No! I mean yes! I mean . . .

ENCOLPIUS   Did you or didn't you try to have it off with him?

ASCYLTOS   Aye, I did. But no I didn't. Have it off. You can't blame me. Look at him, he's as cute as Cupid and he's gagging for it. You'd gone off on one of your public speeches, could have been there for hours. What were we supposed to do? Count three-legged dogs or cats with one eye?

GITON   I saw one this morning. Dog with one eye. Or was it a cat with three legs?

ENCOLPIUS   Go and fuck some whore, not my boyfriend!

ASCYLTOS   It was for his sake, not mine! He was the one who needed to get off. I was just going to help him out. Honest!

ENCOLPIUS   You're unbelievable! You're my best friend. We've known each other since your Mum breast-fed me before she ran off with that Christian.

ASCYLTOS   I thought he was a Mithraite.

ENCOLPIUS   Whatever. Your Dad gave me work minding the pigs. Best job I ever had.

ASCYLTOS   Only job you've ever had.

ENCOLPIUS   We've been pals, mates, buddies all our lives. I've helped you, you've helped me, through thick and thin. And now I've got a boyfriend all of my own, you want to steal him from me.

ASCYLTOS   I don't want to steal him. I just want to share

	him. We share everything else. Why not him?
ENCOLPIUS	He doesn't want to be shared! Do you?
GITON	Well . . . No.
ENCOLPIUS	See, and I don't want to share him. So go and get your own boyfriend or girlfriend or whatever. Selfish prick.
ASCYLTOS	Aye, well, all pricks are selfish, aren't they? We just follow where our pricks lead, do what they tell us. And my prick was telling me . . .
ENCOLPIUS	Okay, okay, okay. Put your prick away and let's forget it.
ASCYLTOS	I can't forget my prick. That's the fucking point!
ENCOLPIUS	Oh, Ascyltos, my brother, I can't stay mad at you.
ASCYLTOS	I can't either. Friends?
ENCOLPIUS	Friends.
ASCYLTOS	Giton?
GITON	Whatever.
	You going to finish that bread?
TRYPHAENA	Hello, boys. New in town?
ASCYLTOS	No.
ENCOLPIUS	Yes.
TRYPHAENA	It's a bit confusing when you first get here, but you'll soon find your way around.
	You wouldn't be gladiators, by any chance?
ENCOLPIUS	Well, I've always . . .

ASCYLTOS	No, we're not.
LICHAS	I'm sure you've seen action in the ring.
ASCYLTOS	Whose ring?
ENCOLPIUS	Actually, we're students.
TRYPHAENA	You must be very bright.
ENCOLPIUS	You could have heard me yesterday, in the Forum.
TRYPHAENA	What were you doing there?
ENCOLPIUS	Giving a lecture. About modern education.
TRYPHAENA	It must have been fascinating.
ENCOLPIUS	Agamemnon joined in.
LICHAS	Agamemnon, father of Electra, her of the Electra Complex who wanted to kill her mother and marry her father, that Agamemnon?
ALL	NO!
TRYPHAENA	We should introduce ourselves. This is Lichas.
ENCOLPIUS	Lichas, the slave who killed the demi-god Hercules by bringing him a poisoned tunic?
LICHAS	No. I own that ship in the harbour.
ASCYLTOS	Impressive.
TRYPHAENA	And I'm Tryphaena.
ENCOLPIUS	The Ptolemaic princess, daughter of the Egyptian Pharaoh who married King Antiochus of Syria?
GITON	Stop showing off.
TRYPHAENA	A distant relative.

ENCOLPIUS   Must be; she's been dead a hundred years.

TRYPHAENA   And you are?

ENCOLPIUS   Encolpius.

ASCYLTOS   Ascyltos.

TRYPHAENA   And this Ganymede?

GITON   My name's not Ganymede. It's Giton.

TRYPHAENA   Delighted to meet you, Giton. I see you like baps.

GITON   I like buns too.

LICHAS   There's a coincidence. So do I.

GITON   First thing I remember is chewing my Mum's baps, first one, then the other. I like them when they're wet and sticky.

TRYPHAENA   You must try mine sometime.

LICHAS   You look as if you go to the gymnasium.

ENCOLPIUS   I go when I have time.

LICHAS   You must have a good set of muscles on you. Stand up. Show me. Nice. Come closer.

               Let's see how you work your pelvis. This is the way I do it. Look . . .

               No, no, that's not right. Like this.

               Change direction, change speed . . .

TRYPHAENA   *(to GITON)* Can you do that? I'd love to see your pelvis working sometime.

ENCOLPIUS finds and removes a pouch from LICHAS' belt.

               What are you doing today, boys? I have a villa

23

	up in the hills, slaves catering to your every need. Why not join us? After you've been to the baths?
ASCYLTOS	We can't afford . . .
TRYPHAENA	A question of cash, is it?
ENCOLPIUS	No, we're fine for money, thanks. We'd love to join you later.
LICHAS	Of course you will. Or I'll know the reason why.
TRYPHAENA	Tryphaena's place. Ask anyone. They'll direct you. We'll lay on dinner. And then we'll lay . . . Well, we'll see.
LICHAS	That's settled then. My dear, shall we go?
TRYPHAENA	Till later, Ganymede. You two as well.
ASCYLTOS	What the fuck was that about? She was going to give us money!
ENCOLPIUS	They already have given us money. Look! There's enough in there to feed us for a month.
ASCYLTOS	Or him for a couple of days.
ENCOLPIUS	We'd better get out of here before they come back.
GITON	What's that? *(a robe)*
ASCYLTOS	They must have left it. Good quality.
ENCOLPIUS	Grab it and let's go!
INNKEEPER	What were you thinking?
PETRONIUS	Excuse me?
INNKEEPER	You were watching them. You weren't happy.

PETRONIUS   I was trying to remember.

INNKEEPER   Remember what?

PETRONIUS   If I wrote that bit.

INNKEEPER   What bit?

PETRONIUS   That bit - Lichas and Tryphaena picking up the boys. So much of my work was lost. Other writers just fill the gaps with whatever comes into their heads.

INNKEEPER   So you're Petronius!

PETRONIUS   Yes.

INNKEEPER   I've been longing to meet you.

PETRONIUS   It feels like my work, but I'm not sure.

INNKEEPER   You're the one telling these stories.

PETRONIUS   Most of them.

INNKEEPER   I've got a question.

PETRONIUS   What is it?

INNKEEPER   What about me?

PETRONIUS   What about you?

INNKEEPER   What happens to me, the innkeeper?

PETRONIUS   Happens? Nothing.

INNKEEPER   Nothing?

PETRONIUS   No, you just slip back into the background and we never hear from you again. Well, not the innkeeper. We see the actor again.

INNKEEPER   Have I got a name?

PETRONIUS   No.

INNKEEPER   A gender?

PETRONIUS   Does it matter?

INNKEEPER   Not really, but it still isn't fair.

PETRONIUS   What isn't?

INNKEEPER   All these characters come in then disappear and you wonder what happens to them and you never know.

PETRONIUS   It can't be helped. You can't tell everyone's story.

INNKEEPER   Like the slaves.

PETRONIUS   What slaves?

INNKEEPER   The slaves at Tryphaena's house. The ones who cater to every need. Will we meet them? Get to know their names? What their lives are like?

PETRONIUS   No, they won't appear. They're just slaves.

INNKEEPER   So they're not important. Slaves are never important.

PETRONIUS   Oh they are, but not to this story. To themselves, to someone else. There'll be other slaves.

INNKEEPER   Will we hear their stories?

PETRONIUS   Maybe.

INNKEEPER   Their names?

PETRONIUS   I'm not sure.

INNKEEPER   But whatever happens, people'll remember you.

PETRONIUS   Yes.

INNKEEPER   Just for telling stories.

PETRONIUS   And for my work for the Emperor. And for the way I die.

INNKEEPER   Ah.

PETRONIUS   It's time for you to go. A bit of advice. Next time, serve fresher bread.

INNKEEPER   But there isn't going to be a next time.

PETRONIUS   No. Pity about that.

SCENE 6: A FOREST

ENCOLPIUS   I need a rest.

GITON   I'm hungry.

ENCOLPIUS   You're always hungry. We've got no food.

GITON   Is there anything to eat in this silent, dark and deserted forest?

ENCOLPIUS   Why are you telling me we are in a silent, dark and deserted forest?

GITON   Don't know. Just seemed the right thing to say. We are in a silent, dark and deserted forest, aren't we?

ENCOLPIUS   Stop saying that.

GITON   Sorry.

I'm hungry.

ENCOLPIUS   Stop saying that too.

GITON   I'm a growing boy.

ENCOLPIUS   Stop fucking growing! As soon as we get out. . .

GITON   . . . of this silent, dark and deserted forest . . .

ASCYLTOS   Say that one more time and you'll regret it.

GITON   Thought you might have forgotten.

ENCOLPIUS   As soon as we get out, I'll buy you something to eat.

ASCYLTOS   Not my size. *(the robe)* Might fit you. Try it on.

ENCOLPIUS   Does my bum look big in this?

GITON   No.

ENCOLPIUS   Pity.

MATE   They went that way!

GITON   What's that?

LICHAS   When I get my hands on him . . .

ASCYLTOS   Sounds like Lichas.

ENCOLPIUS   He's not alone. I don't believe it. They followed us. Let's get out of this . . .

GITON   . . . silent, dark and . . .

LICHAS   We've lost them. When I catch him . . .

MATE   Nice piece of cloth was it, cap'n?

LICHAS   Indian cotton. Well, I'll buy her another. Shame. He was a good-looking lad, that Encolpius. Face of an angel. You wouldn't believe he was capable of theft.

MATE   You said there were three.

LICHAS   Encolpius was the ring-leader. The other two were nobodies. A boy, not bad-looking; Tryphaena couldn't keep her eyes off him. The third one, Ascy-something, half-witted, all body, no brain.

MATE   Can't trust landlubbers, I always say.

LICHAS   Well, I give up. Take the rest of the day off. See your girl.

MATE   Thank you, cap'n.

MATE picks up tunic ENCOLPIUS left behind and exits

LICHAS realises his pouch is missing

LICHAS   The bastard! When I get my hands on him...!

SCENE 7: A MARKET

PETRONIUS   What can I say? I spent hour after hour, day after day, scratching stories onto papyrus and less than half my work survived. All that's left is an episode here, an episode there. At least I know happens next, because I definitely wrote it. We're in a marketplace. Different town, same town? Don't remember. Doesn't matter, does it?

ASCYLTOS   You look ridiculous. Take it off.

ENCOLPIUS   It's cold.

ASCYLTOS   It's the middle of summer.

ENCOLPIUS   I'm cold.

ASCYLTOS   No, you're not. You're shy.

ENCOLPIUS   I'm not shy. My nipples are.

ASCYLTOS   This is ancient Rome, for fuck's sake. No-one's nipples are shy. If they are, put on your tunic.

ENCOLPIUS   I don't have it.

ASCYLTOS   What?

ENCOLPIUS   I left it in the forest when we had to run.

ASCYLTOS   But you kept the gold.

ENCOLPIUS   Uh . . .

ASCYLTOS   For fuck's sake! We've got no money?

GITON   I'm hungry.

ASCYLTOS   That's all we need.

GITON   More than hungry. I'm starving.

ENCOLPIUS	What're we going to do?
GITON	I could die of hunger. Right now.
ASCYLTOS	Go back and look for the tunic?
GITON	You wouldn't even notice.
ENCOLPIUS	We'd never find it.
GITON	Or I could steal some food.
ASCYLTOS	What do you suggest?
GITON	We could sell the robe.
ENCOLPIUS	We've got to think.
ASCYLTOS	You could sell your arse. Wouldn't get much for it.
ENCOLPIUS	Thanks a bunch!
GITON	Sell the robe?
ASCYLTOS	Sell his arse. Worth a bit more.
GITON	How much do you think?
ENCOLPIUS	No! You're not selling his arse or any other part of him. Any more bright ideas?
GITON	We could sell the robe.
ASCYLTOS	Let me think.
ENCOLPIUS	We'll be here all day.
GITON	Why not sell the robe?
ASCYLTOS	We'll sell the robe!
ENCOLPIUS	Sell the robe? Great idea! Why didn't I think of that?
GITON	I've no idea.

ASCYLTOS	Give it here.
ENCOLPIUS	I'll model it.
ASCYLTOS	Give it here!
DORIS	When are you off again?
MATE	Back to sea? In a couple of days. Why?
DORIS	Will you bring me something?
MATE	Maybe.
DORIS	A gold ring?
MATE	You must be joking.
DORIS	Why are you keeping that tunic?
MATE	Thought I'd flog it.
DORIS	Who'd buy it? It's filthy.
MATE	Someone might want it.
ASCYLTOS	*(pointing to the tunic)* Look!
ENCOLPIUS	Ye gods!
GITON	Food?
ENCOLPIUS	Not yet . . .
ASCYLTOS	It's still there! *(the pouch)*
ENCOLPIUS	We've got to get it back before he finds it.
GITON	So your nipples can hide again.
ENCOLPIUS	So that you can get some baps. I'll get your buns later.
[DORIS	Here, is that your captain?
MATE	No, coincidence. A lot of people round here look the same as a lot of others. Someone told

me I look like Agamemnon.

DORIS Who's he?

MATE Agamemnon? Father of Electra, her of the Electra Complex . . . Never mind.]

ASCYLTOS How are we going to get it back?

ENCOLPIUS Ask for it. It's mine.

ASCYLTOS They won't just give it to you.

ENCOLPIUS Why not? They took it. It's mine. The law's on my side.

ASCYLTOS Who's going to believe us? No-one knows us here.

ENCOLPIUS I have an honest face.

ASCYLTOS You have a stupid face. The law's no use. You have to bribe the judge.

GITON Buy it off them.

ENCOLPIUS We've got no money!

GITON I thought you were selling the robe.

ASCYLTOS Forgot about that. Pure cotton. Price was three denarii. Today only two denarii. Once in a lifetime offer. Beautiful piece of Egyptian clothing. Only one and a half denarii . . .

MATE Hold on. Where did you get that robe?

ASCYLTOS Uh... Present. Got it from an admirer.

MATE No you didn't. That belongs to my master, Cap'n Lichas.

ASCYLTOS Never heard of him.

MATE I'll have it back.

ASCYLTOS	Get your hands off!
DORIS	It's ours!
ENCOLPIUS	That's mine!
MATE	What is?
ENCOLPIUS	That tunic. Give it to me.
MATE	It's mine. I found it.
ENCOLPIUS	Where?
MATE	In a silent, dark and . . .
ENCOLPIUS	Got you! It's mine.
VEG SELLER	What's going on here?
DORIS	Who are you?
VEG SELLER	The name's Asparagus. I sell vegetables.
MATE	This pair have stolen my cap'n's robe.
ENCOLPIUS	They've got my tunic I want it back.
DORIS	Thieves, all of them.
ASCYLTOS	We'll be on our way as soon as we get our tunic back.
ENCOLPIUS	My nipples are cold.
MATE	It's our robe!
DORIS	Look at that one - shifty eyes.
GITON	It's true about his nipples.
ASCYLTOS	That's our tunic!
MATE	Give it here!
ENCOLPIUS	Can I have it, please?

BYSTANDER You two want that old tunic and you two want that new robe?

ASCYLTOS, ENCOLPIUS, MATE, DORIS Aye! / Yes!

SELLER You really want that old, dirty, smelly, piece of clothing that looks as if it has wiped several arses and the gods know what else?

ASCYLTOS, ENCOLPIUS Yes!!

BYSTANDER No accounting for taste.

BYSTANDER Or smell.

SELLER Why?

ASCYLTOS Well, you know.

VEG SELLER I don't.

ASCYLTOS You explain.

ENCOLPIUS Because it's . . . You explain.

GITON Because I'm hungry!

SELLER And you're going to eat it? You poor boy.

GITON Yes. No. Because it's got . . .

ASCYLTOS . . . sentimental value!

ENCOLPIUS That's right, sentimental value. You see, his Dad set me to work with the pigs.

ASCYLTOS Fattest pigs this side of Pompeii.

BYSTANDER Smelliest too, it seems.

ENCOLPIUS And he gave me that tunic when I was but a lad.

ASCYLTOS Four years old, weren't you?

SELLER Four years old? A bit big for you, wasn't it?

ENCOLPIUS   He said I'd grow into it.

ASCYLTOS   And he has.

BYSTANDER   What about this robe?

MATE   It belongs to my captain. [You look just like him.

BYSTANDER   Do I? He's a lucky man.]

SELLER   You don't mind giving it them?

ASCYLTOS   Well . . .

ENCOLPIUS   If we get . . .

SELLER   And you'll give them that tunic.

MATE   Suppose we could.

SELLER   So all's well then.

VEG SELLER   Hold on there.

MATE   What?

VEG SELLER   I work for the night watch.

ASCYLTOS   It's not night time.

VEG SELLER   It is now.

BYSTANDER   I thought you sold vegetables.

VEG SELLER   I'm plain-clothes.

SELLER   I always wondered about him. Couldn't tell his artichokes from his aubergines.

ASCYLTOS   For fuck's sake. Just give us the tunic and we'll go.

VEG SELLER   Can't do that. According to regulation M M X X I I I, sub-section S P Q R, where there is a dispute over ownership all pertinent and pertaining items must be brought before a pertinent and pertaining magistrate. And according to paragraph gluteus maximus of the Moronic Code, I have the power to arrest anyone who objects.

BYSTANDER   I swear he's making it up.

VEG SELLER   In short, I have to confiscate both items to present at court tomorrow and I need you all as witnesses.

DORIS   I can't be there.

MATE   Why not?

DORIS   Bacchus and Priapus. Big ceremony.

ENCOLPIUS   Favourite gods of ours, those two. Maybe we'll see you there.

DORIS   No, you won't. Women only, no men allowed.

VEG SELLER   That's enough. Hand over the garments.

ASCYLTOS   For fuck's sake, bribe him!

ENCOLPIUS   With what?

ASCYLTOS   The money in the tunic.

ENCOLPIUS   I haven't got the fucking tunic! That's the whole point.

             Will you listen to reason?

VEG SELLER   How much is reason willing to pay?

ASCYLTOS   Can we pay in instalments?

MATE   Lichas won't like it.

ENCOLPIUS   I'm sure there's a reasonable . . .

GITON	Just take it.
VEG SELLER	Hand them over or . . .
SELLER	The tunic's got to be his.
VEG SELLER	. . . in the name of the law . . .
ASCYLTOS	You knee him in the balls . . .
GITON	Just take it!
SELLER	It stinks too much to be anybody else's.
ASCYLTOS	. . . throw the robe over his head and I'll grab it.
ENCOLPIUS	Knee who in the balls?
GITON	Just take it!!
VEG SELLER	. . . I arrest you all.
GITON	For fuck's sake!

GITON snatches the tunic from the MATE and runs off . Melee in which robe and tunic are thrown from hand to hand and chased by the VEG SELLER until MATE retrieves the robe and exits with DORIS while ASCYLTOS, ENCOLPIUS and GITON exit with the tunic. The VEG SELLER collapses.

SELLER	*(to VEG SELLER)* You all right?
SELLER	That made my day.
SELLER	Better than the circus and no animals hurt.
BYSTANDER	You lost a bap.
SELLER	I've still got a couple.
BYSTANDER	Firm and round?
SELLER	And nice and warm.

BYSTANDER   I'll buy them.

SCENE 8: NIGHT WORSHIP

PETRONIUS   I put that scene in for the Emperor. He enjoyed slapstick.

A misunderstood young man, Nero. Good-looking, sensitive, interested in the arts. Decent singing voice. Even wrote poems. They weren't bad.

Problem was, he became Emperor too young. Sixteen. Didn't know how to rule. Thought if he threw them bread and circuses everyone would be happy. Worked for a while but . . .

Now, he's remembered as mad and vicious. Killed his mother, rejoiced when Rome burned. That's not true - he tried to save the city. As for killing his mother, well, he had his reasons. We all do.

Next: Bacchus and Priapus. The god of wine and the god of fertility. Bacchus, fat, drunk and falling off a donkey. Priapus, with the enormous genital organ.

Some men say it's a torture because it never goes down. Some men say it's a blessing because it never goes down. Women, I believe, are equally divided on the matter.

Once a year, women worship Bacchus and Priapus in secret. Men don't know what goes on at these ceremonies but many are keen to find out.

MAN   You all get naked, don't you?

QUARTILLA   None of your business.

41

MAN   And drunk?

DORIS   Perhaps.

MAN   And you dance.

WORSHIPPER   It's a religious ceremony.

MAN   With your tits bobbing about.

                   Can I come?

WORSHIPPER   No.

MAN   I'll keep very quiet.

WORSHIPPER   No.

MAN   I won't tell anyone.

WOMEN   No!

MAN   I could come if I were a woman.

QUARTILLA   Yes.

MAN   So I am a woman.

WORSHIPPER   No you're not.

MAN   Yes I am.

DORIS   No, you're not.

MAN   If I say I'm a woman, I'm a woman. It's the law.

WORSHIPPER   No, it isn't.

MAN   Well, it should be. Otherwise you're discriminating against me. I insist on coming with you. As a woman. Definitely a woman. Not a man.

QUARTILLA   Come if you want. Call yourself what you like. And if we women see you, I promise you'll come home not so much as a woman but much less of a man.

(the ceremony begins)

QUARTILLA	Bacchus, we drink to you
WORSHIPPERS	While you live you give us hope
ALL	Bacchus! Bacchus! Bacchus! Bacchus!
ENCOLPIUS	Let's go.
ASCYLTOS	Where?
ENCOLPIUS	To join them!
ASCYLTOS	You heard what they said!
ENCOLPIUS	Come on! It'll be fun.
ASCYLTOS	I know what they do to men they catch. I want to stay a man a few years longer.
ENCOLPIUS	Come on! A bunch of women. You big and strong, me a gladiator. No contest.
ASCYLTOS	You a gladiator? After what happened with the trident?
ENCOLPIUS	That only happened once!
	Imagine - all these women naked.
ASCYLTOS	I am imagining.
ENCOLPIUS	So what are we waiting for?
ASCYLTOS	Not me.
QUARTILLA	Bacchus, we drink to you!
	While you live you give us hope
WORSHIPPER	Guardian of the Countryside

DORIS   Come to our festival

WORSHIPPER   Come among us!

WORSHIPPER   Drink with us!

ALL   Priapus, favour us!

The ritual reaches fever pitch until all fall to the ground. A WORSHIPPER, aware of ENCOLPIUS, gropes him. He screeches.

DORIS   What's that?

WORSHIPPER   A man. I have him.

QUARTILLA   A man!

WORSHIPPER   Punish him!

MAN   *(normal voice)* Castrate him! *(high-pitched)* Castrate him!

DORIS   I know you.

ENCOLPIUS   No, you don't.

WORSHIPPER   Grab him!

MAN   I've got him.

WORSHIPPER   No, you haven't. That's me.

MAN   Oh, right.

QUARTILLA   Sounds like there's more than one man here.

MAN   *(high-pitched)* No, there isn't.

WORSHIPPER   Check!

MAN   I'm fine. Check her.

In the confusion MAN runs off but ENCOLPIUS lingers

WORSHIPPER   Heretics! Blasphemers! May they rot in the underworld!

DORIS	I recognised one of them, Encolpius, hangs around the market.
QUARTILLA	We can deal with him.
WORSHIPPER	Like this? *(cutting gesture)*
WORSHIPPER	Could be a waste of a good man - and it's over so quick.
DORIS	Can't leave him unpunished.
QUARTILLA	There's always the curse.
WORSHIPPER	Not the curse!
QUARTILLA	Yes, the curse. Begin.
WORSHIPPER(S)	Hubble, bubble, toil and . . .
QUARTILLA	Wrong curse!
WORSHIPPER(S)	Sorry.
QUARTILLA	Bacchus lord of song and wine
	Priap' lord of this your shrine
ALL	Hear your faithful servants' prayer
	Our loyalty to you we swear
QUARTILLA	Hear your faithful servants' prayer
ALL	Our loyalty to you we swear.
QUARTILLA	Curse the man who saw us here
WORSHIPPERS	His sacrilege will cost him dear
QUARTILLA	What once stood proud must now lie low
WORSHIPPERS	What once was great must never grow
QUARTILLA	Lust will come but never fire
WORSHIPPERS	Shame will always quench desire
ALL	Curse the man who saw us here
	His sacrilege will cost him dear

45

> Lust will come but never fire
>
> Shame will always quench desire

ENCOLPIUS collapses unconscious

QUARTILLA   The curse is laid.

WORSHIPPER   Will he ever recover?

QUARTILLA   That depends.

DORIS   On what?

QUARTILLA   On how desperate he is to get his manhood back.

WORSHIPPER   Will he suffer?

QUARTILLA   He will suffer. In many unpleasant ways.

WORSHIPPER   He'll think he's going through hell.

QUARTILLA   He doesn't know what real hell is.

WORSHIPPER   Few men do.

SCENE 9: TRIMALCHIO'S FEAST

PETRONIUS That went well.

ACTOR What now?

PETRONIUS I was wondering about that. Originally I had Encolpius's ordeal here.

ACTOR Ordeal?

PETRONIUS To recover his manhood. I think he should wait. Anticipation is half the pleasure. For those watching.

  I think we'll move on to Trimalchio's feast.

ACTOR Sounds like a plan.

PETRONIUS: The guests. We need Seleucus, Phileros, Ganymedes, Echion, Agamemnon . . .

AGAMEMNON I'm here!

PETRONIUS . . . Niceros, Plocamus. Then there're acrobats, slaves, chefs . . .

ACTOR Hold on! There are only [NUMBER] of us. Not enough for all these guests, slaves, entertainment . . .

PETRONIUS It's a feast. Extravagant. It goes on for hours. There's music, there are dancers.

ACTOR Can't be helped. Two or three guests maximum, a couple of slaves, no entertainment.

PETRONIUS No entertainment? What about food? We have, in no particular order, sausages, damsons, dormice...

The ACTORS read his manuscript.

ACTOR	peahen eggs . . .
ACTOR	winged hare, a boiled calf . . .
ACTOR	whole wild boar stuffed with live birds,
ACTOR	suckling piglets . . .
ACTOR	garnished pork, oysters, scallops, snails . . .
ACTOR	We won't get half of that.
PETRONIUS	I created a spectacle here!
ACTOR	We'll do our best.
ACTOR	We're Actors.
PETRONIUS	So I've been told.
ACTOR	We can make the audience believe anything.
PETRONIUS	Even in death the gods are punishing me. [Where's Trimalchio?
TRIMALCHIO	Here.
	Fuck off. This is my feast, not for the likes of you.]
	Where's that pisspot Agamemnon? Make yourself fucking useful. Find some guests. Pretty boys. I want fresh arse tonight. Keep me entertained.
AGAMEMNON	As you wish, sire.
TRIMALCHIO	Wife? That all the jewellery you got?
FORTUNATA	It's all you bought me this week.
TRIMALCHIO	It'll have to do.
	You *(SLAVE)*. Pot.

FORTUNATA   Can't you go outside?

TRIMALCHIO   Can't be arsed.

FORTUNATA   At least turn away.

TRIMALCHIO   *(after urinating)* Don't like the look of that. Take it to the oracle. See how long I've got. Make sure she says at least twenty years.

SLAVE wanders into the audience

SLAVE   Can you have a look at this?

TRIMALCHIO   The oracle, I said! That lot wouldn't know what to do with it.

Right, I'm off for a nap.

ENCOLPIUS   A dinner party, you said.

AGAMEMNON   That's right.

ENCOLPIUS   And we're invited?

ASCYLTOS   Why us?

AGAMEMNON   He said he wanted fresh . . .

ENCOLPIUS   Fresh . . .?

AGAMEMNON   . . . meat.

ENCOLPIUS   He wants us to bring fresh meat?

AGAMEMNON   No, he wants you to be . . .

GITON   Will there be lots of food?

AGAMEMNON   Three times as much as you can eat. And Falernian wine.

ENCOLPIUS   The best in the Empire, they say.

ASCYLTOS   And we won't have to pay?

AGAMEMNON	Not with money.
ASCYLTOS	With what?
AGAMEMNON	Entertainment . . .
ASCYLTOS	Another tunic-lifter. I'm not going.
GITON	There's food!
AGAMEMNON	You won't regret it. Trimalchio's feasts are legendary.
GITON	I'm up for it!
ENCOLPIUS	You're always up for it.
GITON	And you're not.
ENCOLPIUS	I was tired.
GITON	Never happened before.
ENCOLPIUS	The richest man in the Empire, you said? And he's inviting us? We have to go.
ASCYLTOS	As long as there's wine.
GITON	And food, lots of food.
ENCOLPIUS	Anything we should know about our host?
AGAMEMNON	He likes flattery. Obsequiousness.
ASCYLTOS	He wants us to grovel.
AGAMEMNON	A bit of grovelling always helps. A lot helps even more.
STEWARD	Welcome, honoured guests.

SLAVE barks loudly; ENCOLPIUS starts

ENCOLPIUS	What was that!?
AGAMEMNON	Watchdog. A slave's cheaper than the real

thing. You don't have to feed it so much.

GITON   He almost pissed himself.

AGAMEMNON   Fortunata, divine beauty! I crave indulgence in bringing to worship at your perfumed feet, Ascyltos, traveller from far off Asturia . . .

ASCYLTOS   Where?

AGAMEMNON   . . . and the scholar Encolpius, who only last week enthralled the Forum with his lecture on modern education, a topic on which I was able to correct his several errors with a little . . .

ENCOLPIUS   Several errors?

FORTUNATA   Who's that?

AGAMEMNON   A minion, divine beauty, servant to Encolpius.

FORTUNATA   A gift for Trimalchio?

ASCYLTOS   I knew it! Another fucking orgy. At least let's eat first.

ENCOLPIUS   Uuhh... This boy is, shall we say, used... I'm sure our host would prefer fresh . . . uh …

ASCYLTOS   . . . meat!

FORTUNATA   Find a place, boys. You don't know when he'll turn up.

GITON   Where do I sit?

ENCOLPIUS   At my feet. You pour my wine and I give you scraps off my plate.

GITON   Thanks a fucking bunch!

TRIMALCHIO enters, stops and farts

TRIMALCHIO   That's better.

	Steward!
STEWARD	Sire?
TRIMALCHIO	Who am I?
STEWARD	You are Gaius Pompeius Trimalchio, the wealthiest man in the Empire.
SLAVE	And one day you will die.
TRIMALCHIO	Make sure it doesn't happen soon.
ENCOLPIUS	His slave told him he was going to die?
AGAMEMNON	Our host has someone tell him once a day to remind him he's mortal.
TRIMALCHIO	Make yourselves at home, lads.
	How's the food?
ENCOLPIUS	Excellent.
AGAMEMNON	Beyond description.
ASCYLTOS	Not bad.
GITON	Don't know. Haven't had any yet.
TRIMALCHIO	And who are you?
ENCOLPIUS	My servant, sir, Giton.
TRIMALCHIO	Come over here, boy.
	Thought I'd bite him, didn't he? Away you go, lad, back to your master. Any time you want to eat, come to me. You two, what are your names?
ENCOLPIUS	Encolpius, sir, at your service.
ASCYLTOS	Ascyltos.
TRIMALCHIO	How much land you got? How many slaves?

Money?

STEWARD   We were told it would be a quiet affair, sire.

TRIMALCHIO   [That fucker Petronius?] Fuck that. I want dancing boys. You *(GITON)* dance for me. Well, come on, show us what you got!

GITON dances but FORTUNATA pushes him aside

AGAMEMNON   She always does this. Thinks she still has a figure. Couldn't dance when she was young and can't dance now she's old and drunk.

TRIMALCHIO   Plonk your arse, wife. Here, boy, come and have something to eat.

GITON   I'm not hungry.

ENCOLPIUS   You're always hungry!

GITON   Not tonight.

TRIMALCHIO   I said, come here, boy! Let's see what you're made of.

FORTUNATA   Dirty dog! Get your hands off him while I'm around. Don't know why you're feeling him. My boobs are bigger than his balls.

TRIMALCHIO   Trouble is, they droop even lower. All right, boy, fuck off back to your master.

ASCYLTOS   What did I tell you?

TRIMALCHIO   Pain in the arse, my beloved wife, but I couldn't do without her. Made her my heir and she's worth every penny.

                 Come on, stuff yourselves! The best food you'll get this year. Everything here comes from my land. Wine's from an estate I bought recently. Don't know where. They tell me it links my property between Rome and Venice. I'm thinking of buying Sicily; nice little place I've heard. They do good lemons.

He farts

I needed that. Haven't shat in days. Doctor's made me eat pomegranates and vinegar. Seems to be working.

He farts

That's better. Any of you need to go, don't hold it in. I've known people die because they were too embarrassed to admit that what goes in has to come out.

You *(SLAVE)*, pot, large one.

TRIMALCHIO defecates

What was it?

SLAVE   Wild boar and uh... quince, sir.

TRIMALCHIO   When did I have them?

STEWARD   The boar three days ago, sir. The quince yesterday.

TRIMALCHIO   That's about right. Meat takes longer. You know what to do with it.

Nothing like a good shit. Empty belly makes room for more food. Dung on the fields gives us food. Which turns into shit again.

AGAMEMNON   Profound, sire, profound.

TRIMALCHIO   But a fucking waste! Why don't we just eat shit and save the hassle of ploughing and harvesting?

AGAMEMNON   Very profound, sire!

TRIMALCHIO   Why don't we eat shit? You *(GITON),* I'll give you ten denarii to eat one of my turds.

Changed my mind. Much better fertilising the asparagus. Tastes good, doesn't it?

Mind you, I have my limits. I never touch the mushrooms. It's where she has her morning piss. Doesn't half smell strong. God knows where it comes from.

Tuck in, everyone. I'll lie down a while. Amuse yourselves.

GITON   I'm still hungry!

ENCOLPIUS   Here you are. We'll go when he's had enough.

ASCYLTOS   Then we'll be here all night.

TRIMALCHIO   You ever been dead?

ENCOLPIUS   Beg pardon, sire?

TRIMALCHIO   You ever been dead?

ASCYLTOS   No-o.

TRIMALCHIO   Me neither. Pity.

ENCOLPIUS   Why?

TRIMALCHIO   I'd like to know what people say about me after I'm gone. Nobody ever tells the truth to my face.

ENCOLPIUS   Why not?

TRIMALCHIO   I wouldn't like it. I'd get upset. I don't like to be

	upset. I prefer being calm, thoughtful.
ENCOLPIUS	Much the best way to be.
TRIMALCHIO	You know how people have - what do they call them? - fancy speeches at the funeral?
AGAMEMNON	Eulogies, sire.
TRIMALCHIO	That's right, eulogies. I won't hear mine.
ENCOLPIUS	That's true.
TRIMALCHIO	I was thinking, have the funeral now, so I can hear what people say about me.
AGAMEMNON	Excellent idea, sire.
ASCYLTOS	Right now?
TRIMALCHIO	Why not?
GITON	You want us to kill you?
TRIMALCHIO	Nah. I'll just pretend to be dead.
FORTUNATA	It would give me some peace.
TRIMALCHIO	Well?
STEWARD	Sire?
TRIMALCHIO	The eu.. the eugory.. the fancy speech! Let's hear it.
STEWARD	From whom, sire?
TRIMALCHIO	All the nobs who come to my funeral.
STEWARD	They're not here, sire. They haven't heard of your unfortunate demise. I'm sure they would be here if they could, sire. Perhaps your wife?
FORTUNATA	He was rich, he was my husband. He's dead. Will that do?

TRIMALCHIO   Say something nice.

FORTUNATA   He didn't beat me.

TRIMALCHIO   How about the stuff I gave you?

FORTUNATA   And he gave me some jewellery. He was conned by the jeweller but he never did have taste.

TRIMALCHIO   You serious? I'll have him whipped.

FORTUNATA   You can't. You're dead.

TRIMALCHIO   Agamemnon. Earn your keep. Say something nice about me. Just the truth. I was the best, that kind of stuff.

AGAMEMNON   Oh, ye deities, cast your omnivident eyes down upon us poor mortals, bereft this day of the epitome, the zenith, the aristos, the earthbound helios . . .

TRIMALCHIO   What the fuck are you on about? Can't understand a fucking word. What's the point of a fancy speech if the dead man can't understand it? You, Enky-what's-your-name. You're eddicated. Say something nice and make sure I fucking understand it.

ENCOLPIUS   Uh... beloved brethren

FORTUNATA coughs

                and sister. We, uh, are, uh, gathered today to commemorate the life and mourn the death of . . . the . . . celebrated, uh . . .

TRIMALCHIO   much-loved

ENCOLPIUS   . . . much-loved, uh, businessman, husband . . . father?

FORTUNATA   Not by me. About two dozen bastards here and there.

TRIMALCHIO   Thirty-seven at the last count.

ENCOLPIUS   . . . prolific father, respected statesman, celebrated philanthropist . . .

ASCYLTOS   host?

ENCOLPIUS   . . . generous host . . .

GITON   pervert?

ENCOLPIUS   . . . lover of youth . . .

AGAMEMNON   . . . sponsor of the arts . . .

ENCOLPIUS   . . . erudite . . .

TRIMALCHIO   What?

ENCOLPIUS   . . . scholar. Loved by all who knew him . . .

FORTUNATA   That's a laugh.

ENCOLPIUS   . . . honest . . .

STEWARD chokes

ENCOLPIUS   . . . a fair master . . .

Scream offstage

. . . whose passing we all grieve. Lucky the gods who welcome him into their midst. A place waits for him at the right hand of Jupiter. Minerva will seek his counsel, Ganymede be his cupbearer, Venus his constant companion, Mars his, uh, his . . .

ASCYLTOS   Bum-boy? Footstool?

AGAMEMNON   Shield-bearer!

TRIMALCHIO	That'll do. I'm getting bored. Why isn't everyone in uncontrollable grief? Shouldn't they throw themselves on my body and beg my soul not to leave them?
STEWARD	Of course, sire.
TRIMALCHIO	Not you! Wife!
FORTUNATA	Must I?
TRIMALCHIO	Second thoughts, no. Had enough of you in life to last eternity. Go count my money. How about the pretty boy?
GITON	Hey, you're supposed to be dead!
TRIMALCHIO	You're right. A stiff can't be stiff. Get off me. How about the slaves? Freedom for any slave who shows his love for me after I'm dead.
AGMEMNON	As an honoured guest for many years, I can do no less.
TRIMALCHIO	Get off me. I can't fucking breathe.
	No respect any of you. You might have killed me.
FORTUNATA	I thought that's what you wanted.
TRIMALCHIO	They'll be fucking dead if they try that again.
	Why so glum? I've come back to life. Celebrate! Let's eat, drink and be merry, for tomorrow we die.
	Not me, of course. I've sacrificed enough oxen at Jupiter's temple to get me another thirty years.
	Agamemnon, tell us a story. A good one.

AGAMEMNON   Well, sire, in your honour, I could . . .

A dish breaks

I could relate . . .

TRIMALCHIO   What was that?

STEWARD   Nothing, sire.

TRIMALCHIO   Don't fuck with me. I know the sound of breaking pottery. Someone broke a fucking plate. Who was it? Tell me now!

ASCYLTOS   I'm sure it was an accident.

TRIMALCHIO   Was it you?

ASCYLTOS   Uh, no.

TRIMALCHIO   Good, because even though you're a guest if you broke a plate I would have your thumbs cut off to remind you not to be so fucking clumsy. Was it one of you?

ENCOLPIUS   I don't think it was. I've been eating from this plate and it's still quite whole and I think I'd know if I . . .

TRIMALCHIO   SHUT THE FUCK UP!

Right, which one of you *(SLAVES)* was it?

Kill them all.

STEWARD   Is that wise, sire? One new slave costs more than a plate. Four would be an extravagance.

TRIMALCHIO   I SAID, fucking kill them all. And you can add yourself if I hear any complaints.

FORTUNATA   There is no point in wasting four slaves.

TRIMALCHIO   I will waste as many slaves as I want. How

60

many have I got?

STEWARD At the last count, sire, one thousand eight hundred and fifty-two male, nine hundred and seventeen female. Not including suckling babes - currently about twenty - and thirty-three with various wounds and ailments who will be disposed of if they do not recover.

TRIMALCHIO So, wife, I can waste four, forty or a hundred and forty of my slaves if I want to. They're my fucking property. I can do what I fucking like with them. Can't I?

STEWARD Indeed, sire.

TRIMALCHIO I can do what I like with you, can't I?

SLAVES Yes, master, of course, master.

TRIMALCHIO So, what's it going to be? One of you or all of you? I ain't got all day. Who dropped the fucking plate?

SLAVE It was me, master.

TRIMALCHIO Come over here, girl. Steward, how much did she cost me?

STEWARD If I remember correctly, sire, she was an infant in a group that you bought with your second farm. She cost you nothing because she was not expected to survive.

The cast freezes

SLAVE (DAPHNE) My name is Daphne.

Like my mother, I have always been a slave. I never knew my father. There were so many men, she said . . .

When she died, I was sent to work in the kitchens. It was hard, but it was warm and I could eat.

I was lucky. The head cook protected me. He did not rape me until I was twelve. He is old and he is not handsome but sometimes he is kind and he lets no other man touch me.

He will buy his freedom next year and he will buy mine and my daughter's too. That is all I want, that is all I ever wanted. To be free.

The cast unfreezes

TRIMALCHIO   How long has she worked for me?

STEWARD   Fifteen years, sir.

TRIMALCHIO   Not bad going if she cost me nothing. The plate, how much was it?

STEWARD   From the third best set, sir. We have many others. A trifle, nothing more.

TRIMALCHIO   Still more expensive than she was. I could have got more use out of it. And I didn't have to feed it. Now it's gone but she's still here and she's useless and costs me money to feed. I'd say I was losing out here.

STEWARD   Yes, sir.

TRIMALCHIO   Crucify her in the morning. Give her to the guards until then.

DAPHNE   No! No! Please, my lord! Spare me! For the love of the gods, spare me!

TRIMALCHIO   You'll meet the gods soon enough.

I'm a fair man, an honest man, a generous

man. Everyone knows that. I respect everyone and they respect me. Look after my property and I'll look after you. Destroy my property and that's the end of you. That's only fair, isn't it? Justice.

Take her away.

DAPHNE   Please sir, I beg you. I have a child.

TRIMALCHIO   That is my child.

DAPHNE   I bore her!

TRIMALCHIO   All children of slaves are mine.

DAPHNE   She needs me!

TRIMALCHIO   Nobody fucking needs you except the guards who need your cunt and your arse and your mouth!

DAPHNE   Set us free! I beg you, set us free!

TRIMALCHIO   You'll be free soon enough.

DAPHNE   My baby! My daughter!

TRIMALCHIO   A girl? Another useless mouth to feed. Throw it to the dogs.

STEWARD   Throw . . . ?

TRIMALCHIO   Throw the brat to the dogs and get this bitch out of my sight.

BLACKOUT

ACT TWO

ACTOR   You all right, love?

(DAPHNE)   I'm okay.

ACTOR   Tough scene, that.

(DAPHNE)   Sometimes I can't get it out of my head. Especially the baby.

ACTOR   Take a rest. We'll finish this.

(DAPHNE)   You sure?

ACTOR   Aye. Come for a drink afterwards.

(DAPHNE)   Might do.

ACTOR   Would do you good.

PETRONIUS   I don´t know where that slave came from. I didn´t create her. I wrote a comedy, not a tragedy. People want to laugh, not cry.

ACTOR   You wrote about life - and all life comes to an end. Sometimes violently.

PETRONIUS   I suppose it does.

     Are we ready?

ACTOR   All yours.

SCENE 10: A LODGING-HOUSE

PETRONIUS   Everyone back? Glasses full, bladders empty? Then I'll begin. We're in another town. Here's Encolpius where you'd expect - in the Forum, lecturing the crowd.

     Back in the lodging-house, Ascyltos and Giton

> are doing what young men do. With a woman, with a man, or on their own depending on what's, so to speak, to hand.

ENCOLPIUS   You!

ASCYLTOS   It's not . . .

GITON   You're back.

ENCOLPIUS   Fuck off! Fuck off now! Get out of here! I never want to see you again.

ASCYLTOS   Come on . . . !

ENCOLPIUS   Who started it? Did you encourage him?

ASCYLTOS   You weren't here.

ENCOLPIUS   That's no fucking excuse! He's my boyfriend. I warned you off him before. Get the fuck out! Now!

ASCYLTOS   It was just . . .

ENCOLPIUS   You were my friend! My brother! My mate, my best pal! We shared everything! Everything! But not my fucking boyfriend!

ASCYLTOS   Well, you haven't been fucking lately, have you?

ENCOLPIUS   That's none of your fucking business!

ASCYLTOS   Your business isn't fucking any more, is it?

ENCOLPIUS   What've you been telling him?

GITON   Nothing!

ASCYLTOS   He doesn't need to. Last time I heard you moan "Jove! Jove! Jove!" was a month ago. The only time I hear him "unh! unh! unh!" is when he's on his own. No wonder he's desperate. I was helping him out!

ENCOLPIUS   Why didn't you stop him?

GITON   He's bigger than me.

ENCOLPIUS   I want you out! Take what's yours and go.

ASCYLTOS   What's mine? Nothing's mine. It's ours. Like you said, we share everything.

ENCOLPIUS   Stop saying that! Take half of whatever and fuck off. Now!

ASCYLTOS   Where's the money?

ENCOLPIUS   It's gone! We spent it. You spent it. Mostly on wine.

ASCYLTOS   Or Giton's baps.

What about him?

ENCOLPIUS   What about him?

ASCYLTOS   We're dividing everything. Half of him's mine. Do we cut him top to bottom or across the middle?

GITON   You're not serious!

ASCYLTOS   Oh, I'm serious.

ENCOLPIUS   Don't be a stupid cunt.

ASCYLTOS   If you're kicking me out and I'm taking half of everything I get half of him.

Nothing personal, you understand.

GITON   No, I don't understand.

ASCYLTOS   Do you want the half with his head or the half

with his cock? Easier than chopping him into left side and right.

ENCOLPIUS   You're not serious. You are serious. I won't let you do this.

ASCYLTOS   Get out of my way.

ENCOLPIUS   Make me.

ASCYLTOS   If I have to.

ENCOLPIUS   You'll have to kill me first. Giton, get me a knife!

ASCYLTOS   Don't make it worse. You'd just cut yourself.

ENCOLPIUS   As long as I get you first.

ASCYLTOS   Get out of the fucking way!

ENCOLPIUS   NO!

GITON   For fuck's sake, stop it! Are you both crazy? Are you going to kill each other then me?

ASCYLTOS   If we have to.

ENCOLPIUS   He's not taking you from me.

GITON   Then kill me!

ENCOLPIUS   What?

GITON   What's the point, friends suddenly enemies? What's the point of anything if you can't trust anybody? One minute you're brothers, best pals, the next you want to kill each other. Or you want to kill me. Why wait? Kill me now! Get it over with. Saves time later. Here's my throat. Come on, both of you stick your knives in. Do it! Fucking do it! Now!

ASCYLTOS   He's right.

ENCOLPIUS   We should kill him?

ASCYLTOS   No, we're brothers. We can't fight. I'm leaving.

ENCOLPIUS   Then go.

ASCYLTOS   Just one thing.

ENCOLPIUS   What?

ASCYLTOS   Giton decides whether he comes with me or stays with you.

ENCOLPIUS   That's easy. He'll stay with me.

                  Won't you?

                  Won't you?

                  No. No! You don't mean it.

ASCYLTOS   His choice. *(to GITON)* Come on.

ENCOLPIUS   Come back. Please. Please. Come back.

SCENE 11: AN ART GALLERY

PETRONIUS   Time passes. A week or two. Encolpius has looked everywhere for Giton but cannot find him. He wanders the town distraught. One day he enters a gallery of art.

EUMOLPUS   By Apelles.

ENCOLPIUS   I'm sorry?

EUMOLPUS   This painting. It's by Apelles. Pliny calls him the greatest of all artists. Of course this is a copy.

ENCOLPIUS   Of course.

              [Have we met before? You remind me of an old woman.]

EUMOLPUS   [How dare you, sir!] My name is Eumolpus.

ENCOLPIUS   Eumolpus the musician, son of Poseidon, God of the Sea and Chione, Goddess of Snow?

EUMOLPUS   Not quite. Eumolpus, son of Horace the butcher and Floris the housewife, itinerant poet.

ENCOLPIUS   Encolpius, son of Anonymous the Unknown and Whoever-it-was, itinerant gladiator.

EUMOLPUS   Where's your trident?

ENCOLPIUS   That only happened once!

EUMOLPUS   You are wondering why I am poorly dressed.

ENCOLPIUS   Uh, no . . .

EUMOLPUS   Merchant and mariner sailing the main
              Risk life to bring back treasure
              General and private fighting in Spain

Return with gold without measure

Flatterers dine with the richest of men

Pimps get rich from lechery

But those of us who live by our pen

Always die in penury.

There was a pun there.

ENCOLPIUS   I noticed.

EUMOLPUS   You were wondering how I live?

ENCOLPIUS   Again, no . . .

EUMOLPUS   I get work as a tutor. I have a reputation, you know.

ENCOLPIUS   I don't doubt it.

EUMOLPUS   My first post . . . You want to hear about it?

ENCOLPIUS   Not partic . . .

EUMOLPUS   I was in Pergamum, lodging with a Treasury official. Boring man with an even duller wife, but a very handsome son in the flower of youth.

Unfortunately, the parents disapproved of the Greek tradition of intimate liaisons between pupils and their tutors. You see the problem...

ENCOLPIUS   I . . .

EUMOLPUS   . . . and you want to hear how I solved it.

I had a cunning plan. I insisted that such relationships offended me. The boy's mother was so impressed by my principles that she begged me to safeguard her son's virtue, accompanying him everywhere and even sleeping in his room.

ENCOLPIUS   I can imagine what followed.

EUMOLPUS   No, I had no wish to take by force. Pleasure should not be taken if pleasure is not also given. One night when my beloved's eyes were closed but I knew he was awake, I prayed aloud to Venus; if I might kiss the youth without his noticing, the next day I would give him two turtle-doves.

The boy feigned sleep. My lips chastely brushed his. In the morning I purchased his doves - and I was not surprised that he expected my gift.

That night I appealed to Cupid, if I may might caress his body without his waking, I would give him two fighting cocks.

ENCOLPIUS   An appropriate gift.

EUMOLPUS   I never thought of that.

Anyway, to indicate his willingness, the youth began to snore loudly and flung his arms out wide. You can imagine what followed.

ENCOLPIUS   Unfortunately, I can.

EUMOLPUS   The next morning he was awake before me and impatient to receive the birds that he - in theory - did not know about. The gods are wise, I told myself, for both youth and tutor are reaping rewards.

The third night, I promised Lord Jupiter that if I achieved my ultimate goal, I would give the boy a Macedonian thoroughbred. Again the young man feigned sleep. I was in ecstasy! The next morning, however, I realised that any horse was far beyond my means and I returned from the market empty-handed.

ENCOLPIUS   And that was that. Your secret was out, the boy was disappointed, he told his parents and you were dismissed.

EUMOLPUS   No, he said nothing. Perhaps, I thought, my seduction had not been in vain. And for several nights I begged to repeat the experience. But each time he said "Go to sleep or I'll tell my father."

ENCOLPIUS   And that was that.

EUMOLPUS   No, temptation was too strong. One night I forced myself upon him.

ENCOLPIUS   Lucky boy.

EUMOLPUS   At first he cried out "Stop or I'll tell my father." but such was my skill in love I brought us both to the highest peak of pleasure.

ENCOLPIUS   And that was that.

EUMOLPUS   Would that it had been. He complained. "What will my friends say? I told them about the first gifts you gave me. Now they'll laugh because you take my body and give nothing in return."

ENCOLPIUS   It is the Roman way.

EUMOLPUS   "I'm a poor tutor." I told him. "I can't afford anything more."

ENCOLPIUS   So he told his father.

EUMOLPUS   No, he asked me to give him something that

cost me nothing.

ENCOLPIUS   What?

EUMOLPUS   To do it again. I was tired but the boy was of an age that never tires of Cupid's caresses. He insisted. I can't, I said. If you don't, he threatened, he would tell his father. And so I gave in and worked hard and we both reached ecstasy again. "Now let us sleep," I said, but he . . .

ENCOLPIUS   I can guess.

EUMOLPUS   "Do it again," he said, "or . . . "

ENCOLPIUS   He would tell his father.

EUMOLPUS   So I did what women often do and pretended joy. He was satisfied. At last, I thought, I could sleep but . . .

ENCOLPIUS   Is there an end to this story?

EUMOLPUS   He wanted it a fourth time, but I had had enough. "Go to sleep," I told him. "if you don't, I'll tell your father."

EUMOLPUS   I have many more such stories. Once I . . .

ENCOLPIUS   I like this statue.

EUMOLPUS   The sack of Troy. Let me explain it to you. In verse.

ENCOLPIUS   Must you?

EUMOLPUS   In tired Troy ten years have passed
since Greece besieged the city.
A wooden horse with wooden arse
appears and looks quite pretty.

Priest Laocoon cries "send it back!"

His sons stand side by side.

Then from the sea, heaving black,

on waves two serpents ride,

entwine the three in fearful death

and something something something breath.

I've forgotten that line. Anyway, it continues …

ACTORS   Do we have to hear this? / The same rubbish every day. / Gives me a headache. / Get out. / *etc*

SCENE 12: A BATHHOUSE

PETRONIUS   Eumolpus always makes me laugh.

ENCOLPIUS   I'm not in the mood.

            I still can't find him. Get him back for me.

PETRONIUS   Giton? I can't help you. I don't know where he is. Characters take on a life of their own, make their own decisions. I merely observe.

ENCOLPIUS   Why did you write The Satyricon?

PETRONIUS   To make people laugh. Show them how ridiculous the Trimalchios and Fortunatas and Eumolpuses of the world are.

            And vanity.

ENCOLPIUS   Vanity?

PETRONIUS   The Satyricon was my Odyssey. Men on an endless journey but with no heroes or villains, no monsters or gods. Just life. In the gutter, not the stars.

ENCOLPIUS   I don't want the stars or the gutter. I just want Giton.

PETRONIUS   Ah, but does he want you? He's young, needs to see the world.

ENCOLPIUS   He can see the world with me. Without him, I'm nothing.

ACTOR   We're getting bored over here. Can we forget the self-pity?

ENCOLPIUS   It's my story! Self-pity is part of who I am. Have you never been in love?

ACTOR	Love is it, or lust?
ENCOLPIUS	A bit of both, I suppose.
ACTOR	Fucking get on with it!
ENCOLPIUS	If it gets me back Giton . . .
ACTOR	Which scene is it?
PETRONIUS	Let's make it the bathhouse.
ACTOR	Why the bathhouse?
PETRONIUS	It's where men meet, do business of every kind. Women too, sometimes, of little modesty. Sooner or later, everyone goes to the bath-house.
ENCOLPIUS	Giton!
	You all right?
GITON	No.
ENCOLPIUS	What's wrong?
GITON	Take me back!
ENCOLPIUS	Why? You wanted to go with him.
GITON	Only because . . .
ENCOLPIUS	Because I can't get it up.
GITON	No! Well . . .
ENCOLPIUS	And he can get it up.
GITON	Yes.
ENCOLPIUS	So you're happy, fucking all day long.
GITON	No! He's rough and selfish and too big and doesn't care if he hurts me or if I get off.

ENCOLPIUS   But you chose him over me.

GITON   I had to.

ENCOLPIUS   Because he's fun to be with.

GITON   No! Well, he is, but that's not why.

ENCOLPIUS   Because he protects you.

GITON   No.

ENCOLPIUS   Because he's got a bigger prick.

GITON   No! Well, he does, but I prefer yours.

ENCOLPIUS   Because underneath that rough exterior there's a sensitive soul who loves nothing better than discussing poetry and theatre and satire and music.

GITON   No!

ENCOLPIUS   Then why?

GITON   Because if If I hadn't gone with him, he would have killed you.

ENCOLPIUS   No, he wouldn't.

GITON   He would. You saw the knife.

ENCOLPIUS   I've known him for years. He's not like that.

GITON   You saw how angry he was. I was afraid.

ENCOLPIUS   So afraid that a fortnight later you're still with him.

GITON   Where else was I to go?

ENCOLPIUS   What're you doing here?

GITON   Waiting for him. He's wrestling with some Greek and I have to scrape the oil off him. Take me with you. Please!

ENCOLPIUS   You hurt me so much. I should fucking hate you.

GITON   I'm sorry. I'll never do it again.

ENCOLPIUS   Promise?

GITON   Promise.

ASCYLTOS   Where is he? Where the fuck is he?

ENCOLPIUS   That's him. Choose. Now. Him or me.

GITON   You. Only you.

ASCYLTOS   Giton, get your arse in here now!

EUMOLPUS   In tired Troy ten years have passed

since Greece besieged the city.

A wooden horse with wooden arse . . .

ACTORS   SHUT UP!

ENCOLPIUS   Which way?

GITON   It's this way.

ASCYLTOS   Gitoooon!!!

EUMOLPUS   *On* the waves two serpents ride,

entwine the three in fearful death

ACTORS   SHUT THE FUCK UP!

EUMOLPUS   Philistines!

CONSTABLE   And don't come back unless you want your tongue cut out!

ASCYLTOS   Where did he go?

CONSTABLE   Who? The old man?

ASCYLTOS   No, the boy. My boy, Giton.

CONSTABLE   Didn't see him.

ASCYLTOS   I think I know where he'll be. Do you know
            where I can find a constable?

CONSTABLE   Funny you should ask.

SCENE 13: A LODGING-HOUSE

ENCOLPIUS You all right?

GITON Yes.

ENCOLPIUS You want anything?

GITON No.

ENCOLPIUS Not even food?

GITON No.

ENCOLPIUS You must be ill.

GITON Just tired.

(hammering)

ENCOLPIUS Who's there?

CONSTABLE Open in the name of the law!

ENCOLPIUS What law?

CONSTABLE Kidnapping. I have reason to believe that you have on the premises property belonging to another citizen.

ENCOLPIUS What property?

CONSTABLE A slave by the name of Giton.

ASCYLTOS I know he's in there.

ENCOLPIUS *(to GITON)* Hide!

    He isn't here!

CONSTABLE I need to inspect the premises.

ENCOLPIUS You can't!

ASCYLTOS It's me, your brother!

ENCOLPIUS	I don't have a brother.
ASCYLTOS	Your best pal.
ENCOLPIUS	I don't have a best pal.
ASCYLTOS	Come on! You can't still be mad at me.
ENCOLPIUS	Oh, I can. I fucking well can.
CONSTABLE	Let us in or we'll break the door down.
ENCOLPIUS	All right, come in.
ENCOLPIUS	No-one here. You can see. Bye.
CONSTABLE	Hold on! Whose leg is that?
ENCOLPIUS	Leg? What leg? Oh that leg. It's mine. Spare, in case I break one. Ancient Rome, lots of accidents, never know when a spare leg comes in handy.
CONSTABLE	There are two of them.
ENCOLPIUS	It's good to have a spare of a spare.
CONSTABLE	Is this him?
ASCYLTOS	Aye, I'd recognise that arse anywhere.
CONSTABLE	I arrest you on a charge of kidnapping.
ENCOLPIUS	Hold on! He came here of his own accord, didn't you?
GITON	Yes, I did.
ASCYLTOS	But you'd gone with me, hadn't you?
GITON	Yes, I had.
ENCOLPIUS	But you didn't want to, did you?
GITON	No. I didn't. Want what?

ENCOLPIUS   To go with him.

GITON   Yes, I didn't.

CONSTABLE   Didn't what?

GITON   Whatever. Can I get something to eat?

ENCOLPIUS   Now you're hungry?!

CONSTABLE   Are you pressing charges?

ASCYLTOS   No, I'm not.

CONSTABLE   Good, because I don't have time for this. I have two desperate, hardened, vicious, violent criminals to catch. They are said to be somewhere in the town.

ENCOLPIUS   Anyone we know?

CONSTABLE   Names of Ascyltos and Encolpius.

GITON   These two . .

     ENCOLPIUS kicks him

     . . . These two don't know them.

ENCOLPIUS   What're they charged with?

CONSTABLE   Theft.

ASCYLTOS   Theft?

CONSTABLE   A pouch of gold from sea-captain Lichas.

GITON   I remember that . . .

     ASCYLTOS kicks him

     . . . I don't remember anything.

ENCOLPIUS   Hardened criminals?

CONSTABLE   Either that or idiots. No-one steals from Lichas and lives.

ASCYLTOS   If that's the case, they'll have long gone. Be half way to Gaul by now . . .

ENCOLPIUS   . . . crossed the Channel . . .

ASCYLTOS   . . . and freezing their balls off in Caledonia.

CONSTABLE   If you see them, let me know. There's a reward in it.

GITON   How much?

both ASCYLTOS and ENCOLPIUS kick him

Cause we don't need the money.

CONSTABLE   Well, if everyone's happy . . .

ASCYLTOS   Oh, we are.

ENCOLPIUS   Ecstatic.

GITON   I'm not.

I'm hungry.

ENCOLPIUS   You weren't thinking of betraying us, were you?

GITON   I wasn't thinking.

ENCOLPIUS   That's normal.

GITON   I'm hungry!

ASCYLTOS   That's even more so.

ENCOLPIUS   We've got to get out of here before the Constable comes back.

GITON   Can we eat first? There's an inn on the other side of the street.

ASCYLTOS	Can't be seen together. I'll go and buy something.
ENCOLPIUS	What with?
ASCYLTOS	Found this at the baths.
	Are we all right?
ENCOLPIUS	You and me? I suppose so.
	He *says* you treated him rough.
ASCYLTOS	Didn't mean to. Just my way.
ENCOLPIUS	He's sensitive. Aren't you?
GITON	What?
ENCOLPIUS	You're sensitive.
GITON	Whatever.
ENCOLPIUS	So leave him alone.
ASCYLTOS	All right. I've had my fun. No harm done.
ENCOLPIUS	For me it's more than fun! And I can't!
ASCYLTOS	Still? It'll come back.
ENCOLPIUS	It's in the hands of the gods.
ASCYLTOS	Well, it's not in your hands. I'll get some food. Fried chicken ok? As soon as I get back, we'll leave.

ASCYLTOS exits; hammering at the door

ENCOLPIUS	Who's that?
EUMOLPUS	A wooden horse with wooden arse . . .
ENCOLPIUS	What's he doing here?
	What're you doing here?

EUMOLPUS   I saw you walk off with a handsome young man
- ah, this young man. I was sure he needed
tutoring. My rates are very reasonable and I
disapprove very strongly of any intimacy
between master and pupil.

ENCOLPIUS   You forget, you told me that story.

EUMOLPUS   So I did. That saves time. Young man, your
mother must have been proud to bear you.
The gods must worship nightly at your shrine.
Will you sleep with me - or rather, not sleep
with me? I will fill my poems with your praises.
As your protector and teacher I will follow you
everywhere, even without your permission.

ENCOLPIUS   No! No! No!

GITON   No, thanks.

EUMOLPUS   Ah well, I tried. No matter. I am leaving town
tonight.

ENCOLPIUS   So are we. Where are you going?

EUMOLPUS   I have no idea. There is a ship sailing - the only
one for at least a week and I have decided to
take a cruise. Why don't you join me?

ENCOLPIUS   We can't afford it.

EUMOLPUS   Come as my slaves. I've never had slaves
before.

ENCOLPIUS   It's an idea. You can take two?

GITON   Two?

ENCOLPIUS   Three.

EUMOLPUS   Three slaves? Why not? That makes me a
wealthy man.

ASCYLTOS   What's he doing here?

EUMOLPUS   I came to offer my services.

ASCYTOS   You were in the baths. You weren't very popular.

EUMOLPUS   Ruffians. No concept of high art. You were very popular - at least part of you was.

ENCOLPIUS   He's leaving tonight. On a ship. We can go with him, get out of here.

    One condition. Keep your hands off him.

EUMOLPUS   At my age, if at first you don't succeed, don't bother trying again.

ENCOLPIUS   And you.

ASCYLTOS   At my age, if at first you do succeed, move on to the next challenge.

SCENE 14: LICHAS' SHIP

SAILORS   Come all you fellows that sail on the sea

Hey, ho, blow the man down

Pay close attention and listen to me

Hey ho, blow the man down

I fought with Brutus at Quiberon Bay

Hey ho, see the men drown

Lost many a comrade on that fateful day

Hey ho, see the men drown

It's a short life and brutal on board a ship

Hey ho, let the bell sound

Terrible food and always the shits

Hey ho, let the bell sound

We're only here cause we're down on our luck

Hey ho, bring the boy round

Our balls are on fire and there's no girl to fuck

Hey ho, bring the boy round.

But whatever the hardships that come to be,

Hey ho, blow the man down

There's no finer life than that lived at sea.

Hey ho, blow the man down!!!

GITON   I'm hungry.

ENCOLPIUS I feel sick.

ASCYLTOS	Can the two of you not shut up?
EUMOLPUS	"Our balls are on fire . . . "
	Boys, boys, how are you?
ASCYLTOS	Fine.
GITON	Hungry.

ENCOLPIUS retches

EUMOLPUS	I brought some food.
ASCYLTOS	Where have you been?
EUMOLPUS	Dining at the Captain's table. Excellent food.

ENCOLPIUS retches

	Charming man. Name of Lichas.
ASCYLTOS	Who?
EUMOLPUS	Lady called Tryphaena. Beautiful. One of the richest in the empire.
ENCOLPIUS	Who??!!
EUMOLPUS	Lichas. Tryphaena.
ASCYLTOS	It's Lichas and Tryphaena we're running from!
EUMOLPUS	That's inconvenient.
ASCYLTOS	You're fucking right it's inconvenient.
ENCOLPIUS	We're dead men. Fates, you win!
GITON	Is there any more food?
ASCYLTOS	They must know we're aboard.
EUMOLPUS	No they don't. I said you were Goths. Spoke a weird language with unpronounceable names.

ENCOLPIUS   We've got to get off the boat.

ASCYLTOS   Before you throw up all over me or before they catch us?

EUMOLPUS   We're too far from land. You'd drown. Wait until we reach port. I got you on safely, I'll get you off.

ASCYLTOS   How?

ENCOLPIUS   In a coffin.

ASCYLTOS   Bribe the helmsman. Say one of us is sick and you have to put in to land.

EUMOLPUS   Wouldn't work. Lichas would come to see the patient and spot you at once.

ASCYLTOS   Some sort of disguise. I know. Ethiopians. You're a writer, you have ink. You can blacken us from head to toe.

EUMOLPUS   I don't have enough for three of you.

GITON   Blacken us?! Why not circumcise us and make us Jews? Or bore holes in our ears and we'll all be Arabs? Cover us in chalk so we look like Gauls. Blue so we're Picts? That won't work, black, white or blue, the colour will run.

I know! How about scarring us all over so we're unrecognisable? Or break our legs so we walk funny?

Just throw us overboard. Drowning is quicker.

Anything more to eat?

ENCOLPIUS   Don't mention food!

EUMOLPUS   We'll just have to shave you.

ENCOLPIUS   What?

EUMOLPUS   Shave your skulls - so you really look like slaves. And brand your foreheads.

ASCYLTOS   You're not branding my forehead or any other part of my body!

LICHAS   I had the strangest dream last night. Priapus told me Encolpius was on board my ship.

TRYPHAENA   Anyone would think we had slept together. I dreamt of Neptune. He told me Giton was here.

LICHAS   If I could lay my hands on them . . .

TRYPHAENA   Not Giton. I'm sure he's innocent.

LICHAS   Hypnotised, I was, by Encolpius' good looks. Face of an angel, heart of a demon. Walked away with half-a-year's profits. I'd beat the living daylights out of him then throw him to the fishes.

TRYPHAENA   There was a third one, wasn't there? Ascyltos. A sweet, gentle, harmless soul, obviously out of his depth. Is there more wine?

LICHAS   Here.

TRYPHAENA   Beautiful night. Full moon. Not a cloud in the sky.

EUMOLPUS drops the blade.

LICHAS   What's going on? Someone is shaving on my ship! Men!

TRYPHAENA   About time. I like my men smooth.

LICHAS   No-one cuts hair on a ship! It brings bad luck!

EUMOLPUS	I didn't know that.
ASCYLTOS	Now we find out.
LICHAS	Seize them. Flog them.

In the confusion ASCYLTOS joins the SAILORS

ENCOLPIUS	Ascyltos!
ASCYLTOS	Leave this to me.

ASCYLTOS lashes ENCOLPIUS lightly.

ENCOLPIUS	Ow! I mean AAAAGHHH!
SAILOR	You hardly touched him.
ASCYLTOS	Start light and build it up, I always say.
SAILOR	Got a point.
GITON	Ow!
SAILOR	He's a good-looking lad.
SAILOR	Pity to scar him . . .
GITON	Ow! Ow! Ow! Please stop!
TRYPHAENA	I recognise that voice.
GITON	It hurts!
TRYPHAENA	It's Giton! Giton, my darling!
ENCOLPIUS	That fucking hurt!
LICHAS	That's Encolpius! On my ship!
	Stop! Give me that! *(the whip)* Hold him.
TRYPHAENA	Giton! I've missed you so much.
LICHAS	Eumolpus! They're your slaves?
EUMOLPUS	No, no, no, no. The men I brought on board

were Goths. Big, beefy types. Don't know where these three came from. Must have overpowered my poor, defenceless slaves and thrown them overboard.

LICHAS   Three? Ah yes. You were with them.

ASCYLTOS   Sure it wasn't someone who looked like me? There's a lot of us about.

LICHAS   Let them go.

Where's my gold?

ENCOLPIUS   Gold?

ASCYLTOS   Gold?

EUMOLPUS   Gold?

TRYPHAENA   Gold?

LICHAS   The gold you stole from me.

ENCOLPIUS   I don't remember any gold. Do you remember any gold?

ASCYLTOS   I don't remember any gold.

GITON   I remember . . . *(ASCYLTOS and ENCOLPIUS kick him)* . . . there wasn't any gold.

ENCOLPIUS   That's right, no gold.

ASCYLTOS   There was a robe.

ENCOLPIUS   Yes, a robe. We found a robe. Suited me down to the ground. Just right for my complexion.We gave it back as soon as we knew it was yours.

MATE   You tried to sell it.

ENCOLPIUS   Before we knew it was yours. We would have given you the money. If we'd sold it.

ASCYLTOS	But we didn't. Sell it.
GITON	You got it back.
MATE	After you ran off with it. Thought I'd seen you before.
TRYPHAENA	Giton, you are as honest as you are handsome. Let him go. I vouch for him.
SAILOR	Can I go ahead and flog this one?
SAILOR	Me too!
LICHAS	What for?
SAILOR	Shaving.
SAILOR	Stowing away.
SAILOR	Stealing your gold.
SAILOR	Whatever you like.
SAILOR	Long time since I flogged anyone.
SAILOR	Me too!
SAILOR	Me too!
LICHAS	If anyone flogs anyone it'll be me. It's tempting.
ENCOLPIUS	Never yield to temptation. You never know where it might lead.
LICHAS	I could throw him overboard. All three of them.
TRYPHAENA	Not Giton!
ENCOLPIUS	I'd float. Light as a bubble, me. Wouldn't drown. Not worth it. Any other option? Need an extra galley-slave, perhaps?
ASCYLTOS	Two extra galley-slaves?

EUMOLPUS   Why not pardon them?

LICHAS   Pardon?

EUMOLPUS   Look at them, begging for mercy.

                Free men who allowed themselves to be held
                as slaves. Haven't they suffered enough?
                Starved of food. About to lose their hair. I will
                sing your praises if you are merciful.

LICHAS   If you start singing it'll be you who's flogged.

TRYPHAENA is covering GITON with kisses.

ENCOLPIUS   Get off him!

LICHAS   Get off her!

TRYPHAENA   Get off me!

EUMOLPUS   Surely we can resolve this like gentlemen.

LICHAS   I am resolving it like a gentleman.

GITON   Stop! *(holding a knife against his crotch)*

                Stop or I'll cut it off!

LICHAS   Are you mad?

ASCYLTOS   At least it's not his throat this time.

TRYPHAENA   My darling boy, don't!

GITON   This is what you *(TRYPHAENA)* want, isn't it?
                Well, you won't get it, no-one'll get it, if
                everyone keeps fighting.

TRYPHAENA   You can't disfigure that beautiful body!

ENCOLPIUS grabs the knife from GITON

ENCOLPIUS   Stop or I'll kill myself!

EUMOLPUS   Before or after Giton castrates himself?

ASCYLTOS   For fuck's sake. *(grabs the knife)* Which bit of me should I cut?

LICHAS   I won't let you damage that beautiful body.

ENCOLPIUS   You were having me whipped.

LICHAS   That's different.

ENCOLPIUS   Not to me, it isn't.

ASCYLTOS   What about my beautiful body?

SAILOR   If I flog it, will you hold it against me?

TRYPHAENA   I propose a truce. Do you agree?

EUMOLPUS   I could write out terms.

LICHAS   Don't bother.

EUMOLPUS   Compose a poem?

             "Proud Giton hacks off cock and balls;

             By his side his lover falls."

LICHAS   Not if you value your life.

TRYPHAENA   Let us drink to a truce, then. Where did we leave the wine?

PETRONIUS   And so everyone calmed down. Food was eaten, wine was drunk. Days passed. Giton learnt the arts of love from Tryphaena in her chamber, while Lichas took his pleasure with Encolpius. Ascyltos made friends with and profited from the crew while Eumolpus composed more doggerel.

             And The Ship Sailed On.

             Until the storm came.

SCENE 15: A BEACH

PETRONIUS　　How many lives were lost each year to the sea? Only the gods know. In this case Tryphaena and the sailors survived but are no longer part of our story. Encolpius and Giton found themselves wet but alive on the shore.

ENCOLPIUS　　Drowned. Poor wretch. Perhaps a wife waits for him. Perhaps a son. Or a father. Who loved him? Kissed him last? Where was he going? What was his future?

GITON　　It's Lichas.

ENCOLPIUS　　No.

GITON　　Aren't you glad he's dead? He had you whipped. He beat you. He used you.

ENCOLPIUS　　So now we should celebrate? No man should die before his time. Life is all we have. Without it we are nothing.

　　You Fates, you bastards! Why give us life and hope and then destroy us?

　　We can't leave him like this. He died in water but he will go to the afterlife in fire.

　　An obol for Charon.

　　Sit semper in pace anima tua.

PETRONIUS　　Some live, some die, some disappear.

ASCYLTOS　　What about me?

PETRONIUS　　Ascyltos? I lost interest in you long ago. In my version you weren't even on the ship.

ASCYLTOS　　Yet here I am, alive and kicking. Where do I go

now?

PETRONIUS   No idea. You could follow the others. They went that way.

ASCYLTOS   I have to. Encolpius is my brother.

PETRONIUS   And Giton?

ASCYLTOS   Cute but not my type. I only wanted him to wind up Encolpius.

PETRONIUS   Such is friendship. I wish you luck.

Eumolpus!

EUMOLPUS   I'm on? Which scene is it?

PETRONIUS   You're done. Not needed any more.

EUMOLPUS   Done? But what about my other stories?

PETRONIUS   It's out of my hands.

EUMOLPUS   The Widow and the Soldier. It's so romantic.

PETRONIUS   No time. Gone.

EUMOLPUS   Can't I at least tell it quickly?

PETRONIUS   No.

EUMOLPUS   The one where my creditors turn cannibal?

PETRONIUS   They can watch the film. Just go.

EUMOLPUS   Go where?

PETRONIUS   Into the past. Into imagination. Into nothingness.

EUMOLPUS   "Proud Giton hacks off cock and balls;
by his side . . . "

SCENE 16: CROTON

PETRONIUS   Fortune's wheel keeps turning. Even I could not avoid fate. Once I was Nero's favourite. An emperor should flaunt his wealth and I ensured his entertainments were popular. Some of his wealth even flaunted my way. Then came the fall.

I'm lucky, I suppose. Some of my stories survived. And my ghost lives on, inhabiting whatever body is to hand. This one is not bad. Older and thinner than I was when I died. A bit sepulchral, but better-looking than me. Unfortunately, I can't keep it; the owner wants it back.

Time for one last tale. We are in the market of a town called Croton and our young heroes - let's call them heroes now, they have gone through so much they deserve it - our heroes are doing what lovers always do when love eludes them. They quarrel.

ENCOLPIUS   Where were you?

GITON   Wandering around.

ENCOLPIUS   You could have told me.

GITON   Why? Do you care?

ENCOLPIUS   I worry about you.

GITON   I can look after myself.

ENCOLPIUS   Are you mad at me?

GITON   No.

ENCOLPIUS   Look me in the eye and say that.

GITON	Leave me alone!
ENCOLPIUS	You really want me to?
GITON	Yes. No. I want. . . I want us to fuck! We share a bed but it's like Socrates and Alcibiades: nothing happens.
ENCOLPIUS	So much has been going on. No time. No energy.
GITON	I've got energy.
ENCOLPIUS	Of course you do, you're sixteen!
GITON	I'm . . . ! How old am I?
ENCOLPIUS	You'll always be sixteen to me. And I'm twenty-four. It's not so easy at my age.
GITON	Right(!)
ENCOLPIUS	Besides, you went off with Ascyltos that time. Then there was Tryphaena. I'm sure you've had others - women, men, the gods know what else.
GITON	I'd rather have you.
ENCOLPIUS	And me you.
GITON	So show me! Now!!
ENCOLPIUS	Here in the market?
GITON	There is no market.
ENCOLPIUS	You're right. Where did it go?
GITON	It just disappeared. There's no-one here.
ENCOLPIUS	I don't like people watching. It feels like there are eyes on me.

GITON	There's no-one. We're all alone.
ENCOLPIUS	All right then.
CHORUS	What once stood proud must now lie low
	What once was great must never grow
GITON	Again!
ENCOLPIUS	I'm cursed.
GITON	You keep saying that. Your love should be stronger than any curse.
ENCOLPIUS	No love is stronger than a woman's curse.
GITON	Then you're as weak as a woman. Fuck off.
	Let me go.
ENCOLPIUS	No.
GITON	Let me go!
ENCOLPIUS	Not like this.
GITON	Let me go!!
ENCOLPIUS	I love you! I love you!
GITON	Just words. All I get from you is words. Let me go! Let me fucking go!
	I don't love you. You're weak, pathetic, sexless. There's nothing to love.
ENCOLPIUS	Giton!
GITON	Leave me alone! Fuck off! Just fuck off!
ENCOLPIUS	Fuck, fuck, fuck, fuck, fuck!
CHRYSIS	Good day, young master.
ENCOLPIUS	Good day to you.

CHRYSIS   Cocky young fellow, aren't you?

ENCOLPIUS   Cocky? I wish.

CHRYSIS   I have a customer for you.

ENCOLPIUS   A customer?

CHRYSIS   My mistress. She goes for types like you. Low-lifes. The dregs of society.

ENCOLPIUS   That's flattering.

CHRYSIS   She sees a mule-driver stinking of sweat and the juices start flowing. A hairy bare-arsed kitchen slave covered in grease is her idea of heaven.

ENCOLPIUS   No accounting for taste.

CHRYSIS   Me, on the other hand, I wouldn't touch a slave. I know where they've been. A nobleman, that's my fancy. I won't sit on the lap of anyone who hasn't got a pedigree as long as my arm.

ENCOLPIUS   Do you have much luck?

CHRYSIS   Now and then. Anyway, you wait here.

CIRCE   I am Circe.

ENCOLPIUS   The enchantress and minor goddess who bore the wanderer Ulysses two sons and who can turn men into pigs?

CIRCE   No, just a beautiful woman brought into this story to bring spice into your life.

ENCOLPIUS   So no enchantress, but you are enchanting me.

CIRCE   You are in the market, aren't you?

ENCOLPIUS	We both are.
CIRCE	I mean for a girlfriend. I saw your boyfriend, but that's not a problem is it?
ENCOLPIUS	Boyfriend? What boyfriend? Giton? A passing fancy. Over. Barely remember him.
CIRCE	Don't his lips inflame you, doesn't his body arouse every passion in you?
ENCOLPIUS	Long time ago.
CIRCE	And me? Do my lips inflame you? My body arouse your passion? Take me in your arms. Show me your love.
ENCOLPIUS	We're not alone.
CIRCE	Yes, we are. No-one can see us. The market has gone.
ENCOLPIUS	It has a habit of doing that.
CIRCE	Your beloved boy is nowhere around.
CHORUS	Lust will come but never fire
CIRCE	What's the problem? My kissing? No-one has complained before. My breath? I chewed mint all morning. My underarms? Do you think I didn't wash?
ENCOLPIUS	No, it's . . .
CIRCE	It must be fear of your boy that's keeping you limp.
ENCOLPIUS	Afraid of Giton?
CHORUS	Shame will always quench desire
ENCOLPIUS	I am cursed.

CIRCE   You are cursed? What about me? The time I took to wash and dress this morning, wasted. Because some pansy pretended he could satisfy me. Now I have to sacrifice to Venus to beg her forgiveness.

ENCOLPIUS   You, prick, where've you gone? Traitor! I can hardly see you. No wonder you're hiding. You should be fucking ashamed. Except you're not fucking anything! You've lost me Giton and I can't get you up for a girl. You're dragging me to hell when I should be in heaven. You're making me old when I'm still young. I should cut you off and throw you away.

CHRYSIS   Psst!

ENCOLPIUS   What?

CHRYSIS   My mistress apologises for her temper. She says you are in great danger. If a man cannot respond to someone as beautiful as she, he is as good as dead. She wishes to save you from a life without life.

ENCOLPIUS   How?

CHRYSIS   She bids you come to her tomorrow, but first you must follow these instructions to give you strength.

    Tonight you must eat onions and snail heads without seasoning. Then sleep long and alone. In the morning rise at leisure, oil yourself moderately, do not wash, then return here at this time. My mistress will take you to the temple so you may sacrifice yourself at the altar of love.

PRIESTESS   Is the soldier ready for battle?

ENCOLPIUS   Uh . . .

PRIESTESS   Young man, seek the god's favour.

ENCOLPIUS   Oh, Priapus, son of Bacchus, god of fields and fertility, hear my prayer. Restore my strength, return my manhood. I shall not let your glory go unthanked. I shall sacrifice to you a horned goat, a litter of pigs, a cow with udder swollen with milk. The best wines will flood your temple and drunken young men displaying their virility will march in triumph round your shrine.

PRIESTESS   Amen!

                Unsheath the weapon! Let battle commence!

CHORUS   His sacrilege will cost him dear

                Lust will come but never fire

                Shame will always quench desire

ENCOLPIUS   No! No! Priapus, I beg you!

CIRCE   He is as good as dead.

PRIESTESS   Then we must try the second cure

ENCOLPIUS   The second? What's that?

PRIESTESS   Satyrion. *[not Satyricon]*

ENCOLPIUS   What's in it?

PRIESTESS   Blood of goat, root of mandrake, Spanish fly and tiger's tooth.

                And two bulbs of raw garlic.

ENCOLPIUS   Tasty (!)

PRIESTESS   You must down it in one.

ENCOLPIUS   I'll try anything.

PRIESTESS   Oh Venus, take pity on your acolyte and bestow your grace on this pitiful wretch who seeks to serve her.

CIRCE   Do you feel anything?

ENCOLPIUS   Sick.

PRIESTESS   Do you feel anything?

CIRCE   No.

PRIESTESS   The gods demand more.

ENCOLPIUS   What?

PRIESTESS   Pin him down.

WORSHIPPERS beat ENCOLPIUS with branches

ENCOLPIUS   Aagh!

CIRCE   My poor boy. What torment you are suffering. But it is nothing compared to the torment of my aching, empty thighs.

ENCOLPIUS   Aagh! Your torment is worse than mine?

    Ow!

CIRCE   You have bewitched me. Without your love, without your body I cannot live.

ENCOLPIUS   OW! I'm sure you can. Stop! Please stop!

PRIESTESS   Are you in rut?

ENCOLPIUS   I'm in agony.

PRIESTESS   We are only halfway through the treatment.

ENCOLPIUS   I'm in rut! I'm in rut!

CIRCE — We can see that you are not.

CHRYSIS — He has fainted.

CIRCE — Wake him.

ENCOLPIUS — No more, no more!

PRIESTESS — We need the ultimate cure.

CIRCE — What?

CHRYSIS — What?

ENCOLPIUS — What?

PRIESTESS — This. *(a large dildo)*

ENCOLPIUS — Not that! Not that!

PRIESTESS — Do not worry, it is oiled.

ENCOLPIUS — I'm still worried.

PRIESTESS — With pepper seeds and nettle leaves.

ENCOLPIUS — I'm not hungry!

PRIESTESS — Hold him down.

ENCOLPIUS — This is hell!

CIRCE — He thinks he's in hell.

PRIESTESS — He doesn't know what real hell is.

CHRYSIS — Few men do.

CHORUS — WHAT ONCE STOOD PROUD MUST NOW LIE LOW

WHAT ONCE WAS GREAT MUST NEVER GROW

LUST WILL COME BUT NEVER FIRE

SHAME WILL ALWAYS QUENCH DESIRE

SCENE 17: A LODGING-HOUSE

GITON   You're awake.

ENCOLPIUS   Where am I?

GITON   At home.

ENCOLPIUS   I had a bad dream. Aagh! It wasn't a dream.

GITON   Keep still.

ENCOLPIUS   How did I get here?

GITON   We brought you, me and Ascyltos.

ENCOLPIUS   Where is he?

GITON   Gone.

ENCOLPIUS   Gone where?

GITON   Don't know. He said to seek new adventures.

ENCOLPIUS   He'll be back. Eventually.

            I thought you had left me.

GITON   I'm sorry.

ENCOLPIUS   I wouldn't blame you.

GITON   I won't do it again. I missed you.

            You won't leave me, will you?

ENCOLPIUS   Never.

GITON   Will we have more adventures?

ENCOLPIUS   Of course we will. All our lives will be an
            adventure. Our adventures will never end.

GITON   Promise?

ENCOLPIUS   Promise.

GITON   I need you.

ENCOLPIUS   I need you. But I can't . . .

GITON   Doesn't matter. I can always get it elsewhere.
               There were these two girls yesterday...

ENCOLPIUS   Better if you get it from me.

GITON   Yes.

ENCOLPIUS   What's that noise?

GITON   Young couple. Been at it all day. Lucky sods.
               You can see them through that hole in the
               wall.

ENCOLPIUS   Let me see.

               She's pretty.

GITON   Nothing special.

ENCOLPIUS   What about him?

GITON   Wouldn't say no.

ENCOLPIUS   What's he doing now?

GITON   I think she's got hold of his . . .

ENCOLPIUS   I didn't think anyone could do that.

GITON   I can.

ENCOLPIUS   Since when?

GITON   That time on the ship. Tryphaena taught me.

ENCOLPIUS   Really?

GITON   I wanted to show you, but you . . .

ENCOLPIUS   But I . . . ?

GITON   I didn't know if . . .

	. . . if you . . .
	if you could . . .
ENCOLPIUS	Get it up?
	For a long time I couldn't. But now . . .
	Now . . .
GITON	Now?
ENCOLPIUS	What do you think?
GITON	Definitely. Just like before.
ENCOLPIUS	Better than before! Much better than before! You'll see.
GITON	Show me.
ENCOLPIUS	Thank you, Priapus!

SCENE 18: PETRONIUS' DINNER

PETRONIUS   Ah, youth. Wasted on the young.

              Who are you?

EMISSARY   An emissary from the emperor.

PETRONIUS   How is the boy?

EMISSARY   The emperor Nero is no boy.

PETRONIUS   He's only twenty-six. Compared to me he's a
              boy. He'll be dead by the time he's thirty.

EMISSARY   You are likely to be dead before him. *(hands
              PETRONIUS a document)*

PETRONIUS   Ah. I suspect that oaf Tigellinus has gained the
              divine ear. He was always jealous of me.

ENCOLPIUS   What does it say?

PETRONIUS   Art lasts, life does not.

ENCOLPIUS   What will you do?

PETRONIUS   Do? It is late in the day. Shall we dine?

GITON   Eat?

ASCYLTOS   You haven't stopped stuffing yourself!

GITON   So?

PETRONIUS   Nothing ostentatious. Some wine, good
              conversation. See what's left of Trimalchio's
              feast. Ascyltos, give me a knife.

              Cheer up! We're not at a funeral. My last
              supper should be one to remember. Your
              health, everyone.

              Someone, say something. You, Actors, what

117

	did you think of the stories?
ACTOR	A bit over the top, some of them.
ACTOR	Fun to watch, fun to act.
ACTOR	I'd do it again.
ACTOR	That poor girl. I can't forget her.
PETRONIUS	I don't know where she came from. Too depressing for my tastes.

He cuts his wrists

And Ascyltos on Lichas' ship. Shouldn't have been there. Why did they have to keep changing my story?

ACTOR	You're not the only one. Think how Agatha Christie and that Will Shakespeare feel, the way their work is always mucked about.
ACTOR	Better to be remembered poorly than not remembered at all. Who knows my name? Any of my names?
ACTOR	You're obsessed with sex.
PETRONIUS	It's what brings us into the world.
ACTOR	Not the way you prefer it.
PETRONIUS	True. Imagine if we kept having more and more children until the world overflowed with people.

Encolpius, what did you learn from the stories?

ENCOLPIUS	Learn? Can't think of anything.
PETRONIUS	Not even to steer clear of secret ceremonies?

I'm glad. You will live your adventures again

and again. It's better if you don't remember what happened before.

Giton?

GITON   What?

PETRONIUS   What have you learnt?

GITON   Unh?

PETRONIUS   Perfect. May you remain forever sixteen.

GITON   I'm . . . sixteen! Yes, I'll always be sixteen!

PETRONIUS   As long as you're old enough to enjoy life. That's all that matters.

               Let me enjoy this moment. Bring me cloths.

ASCYLTOS wraps cloths around PETRONIUS' wrists

               Ascyltos? I didn't expect you to be so solicitous.

ASCYLTOS   You didn't, did you? You created me for nothing but fighting, drinking and fucking. But I care for people, look out for them.

               You gave me a huge prick but no love. Encolpius gets Giton. I get men I don't want, almost never get a woman and spend half the time with aching balls and a permanent stiffie. You don't even have me wank and to top it off I disappear!

PETRONIUS   I'm sorry. But look what happens to Encolpius. The agony he has to go through before he gets his manhood back. You wouldn't want that.

ASCYLTOS   Why not? What's pleasure? Sensation. What's pain? Sensation. At least pain tells you you're

119

alive. Give me pain, give me love, give me anything but not oblivion.

PETRONIUS   It's a point of view.

ACTOR   What about us?

PETRONIUS   "Us"? You Actors?

ACTOR   We Women.

PETRONIUS   What about you women?

ACTOR   Your stories are all about men.

PETRONIUS   Not true. There are plenty of women in them.

ACTOR   But men dictate what happens.

PETRONIUS   Again, not true. Tryphaena and Circe took the initiative; plenty of other women did the same.

ACTOR   They still lived in in a man's world.

          How many women are there here? Women are half the world. Women want to hear women's stories. Ordinary women. All you give us are slaves, whores and the rich. How many women sitting in the audience can identify with them?

          What can your stories tell them?

PETRONIUS   Nothing that they don't want to hear.

ACTOR   Why should we? You're just another dead white male.

PETRONIUS   Not yet, but you'll soon get your wish.

PETRONIUS unties the cloths round his wrists. Blood flows

ACTOR   What about trans, non-binaries? You didn't include them.

PETRONIUS   Who?

ACTOR   Transgenders. Non-binary people - not one sex or the other.

PETRONIUS   We didn't have them in my day. Just the occasional hermaphrodite.

ACTOR   That's what you think.

ACTOR   The stories had the ring of truth. Most of the time the men were driven by desire.

ACTOR   Lust.

ACTOR   And gluttony. And avarice. Power.

ACTOR   It all comes down to the same in the end. Be in control. Be on top.

ACTOR   And the women?

ACTOR   Careful!

ACTOR   They used men's desires to achieve their goals.

ACTOR   Maybe they just wanted the same thing - to get laid.

ACTOR   Maybe they had no choice. They were just trying to survive in a man's world.

ACTOR   They didn't all survive.

PETRONIUS   That's all any of us do. Try to survive. We don't always succeed.

ACTOR   What do you think?

ACTOR   Me?

ACTOR   You must have an opinion.

ACTOR   Someone   once   said   only   fools   express opinions; the wise stay silent.

ACTOR   Probably Socrates.

ACTOR   "Let your guide be Socrates,

the wisest man who ever lived."

ACTOR   What about Giton?

ACTOR   What about him?

ACTOR   Forced to have sex with all these men.

ACTOR   And women.

PETRONIUS   Nobody forces him.

ACTOR   He's only sixteen!

ACTOR   And that boy in Eumolpus' story. Stalked and raped.

ACTOR   Sounded like he wanted it. Ask him how he feels.

ACTOR   He isn't here!

ACTOR   So don't assume you know how he feels.

PETRONIUS   Nero became emperor at sixteen. It's not the age, it's the situation. Giton is young, he's free . . .

ACTOR   . . . dumb and full of cum . . .

PETRONIUS   . . . let him do what he wants.

ACTOR   You wouldn't say that if he was a girl.

ACTOR   Why not? Girls want the same as boys, don't they?

ACTOR   Young people should be protected.

ACTOR   The idea of young keeps changing.

ACTOR   Everything changes, all the time. People will look back at these stories and maybe they'll be appalled by what was said and done - or maybe they'll laugh or maybe they'll just wonder at the complexity of human relationships. Some will claim to be guardians of morality and denounce those who went before. What they forget is that the generations who follow them will look back on their lives and see all the injustice and abuse that they don't see.

ACTOR   What are you going on about?

ACTOR   All I'm saying is the present always condemns the past - and the present will be the past one day.

ACTOR   You've gone all philosophical.

ACTOR   Well, what do I know? We're only actors, aren't we? Bring us on when you need us. Put words in our mouths. Then send us home and forget us. But some of us, we watch, we think.

PETRONIUS It's only a story, a collection of stories. From long, long ago. *(dies)*

ENDING A

(if no BACCHUS in scenes 1, 8 and possibly 16)

ACTORS   Ladies, gentlemen, non-binaries, The Satyricon!

ENDING B

(if BACCHUS has appeared in the play)

BACCHUS laughs

Changes

Those familiar with Petronius' classic tale will know which parts have been brought into the play and how much has been left out. Newcomers to *The Satyricon* are advised to read several translations which will indicate how the text can be interpreted. Like this play, many versions include episodes that Petronius never wrote, filling gaps in the original story.

In addition to the invented scenes, some aspects of the play are not found in Petronius. These include Giton's constant hunger, Encolpius' habit of greeting newcomers with the historical or mythological background to their names and the repeated joke about his trident. The idea that he and Ascyltos are foster brothers rather than former lovers is also new and much of the history of the three hinted at or described in the original is ignored. Astute readers will identify many other errors, anachronisms and fabrications. In each case the modern author pleads dramatic licence.

Numbers in **bold** refer to sections of Petronius' text.

SCENE 2: THE FORUM
1 - 5
Difference: the crowd does not join in Agamemnon's poem.

SCENE 3: A STREET AND A BROTHEL
6 - 8
Differences: the old woman is described as a vegetable seller; neither her name nor the Encolpius' landlady's name is given.

SCENE 4: A STREET
part of **9**
Differences: The conversation in the play between Ascyltos and Encolpius is invented. In the original Giton and Encolpius are in

the lodging-house when the boy tells him that Ascyltos alluded to the story of Tarquin and Lucretia in threatening to rape him.

SCENE 5: THE COOKED GOOSE

part of **9** and part of **10**

Difference: Ascyltos' response to Giton's accusation and his and Encolpius' anger turning to laughter comes immediately after Giton's tearful confession.

SCENE 6: A FOREST

The scene is invented. The idea of the tunic being lost in the wood is adapted from apochryphal versions.

SCENE 7: A MARKET

12 - 14

Differences:
* the robe is a cloak that has been stolen; from whom is not stated;
* the source of the money secreted in the tunic is not given;
* the Mate is a country peasant;
* Doris is the name of an old love interest of Encolpius **(126)**;
* the tunic is recovered more easily.

SCENE 8: NIGHT WORSHIP

In **16 - 17** Quartilla, accompanied by her maid, begs that Encolpius and Ascyltos do not reveal the forbidden Priapic rites they have witnessed. The worship itself is not described and there is no mention of a third man. In **20** Encolpius is impotent.

SCENE 9: TRIMALCHIO'S FEAST

26 - 78 comprises the largest surviving segment of Petronius' work. Much of it is taken up with descriptions of the food and conversations with the other guests. Alterations include:
* a slave of Agamemnon's invites the trio to the feast;
* the dog at the entrance to Trimalchio's house is a painting

not a slave;
* Trimalchio, not Fortunata, is born under Cancer;
* Trimalchio considering the idea of eating excrement and suggesting Giton do so is invented;
* Agamemnon, not Ascyltos, introduces the idea of "a poor man";
* there is no mention of Trimalchio being a father;
* Trimalchio pretends to be dead but there is no mock funeral;
* when a slave breaks a plate Trimalchio casually tells him to kill himself before reprieving him at his guests' request (**52**); another slave is mentioned as being crucified because he insulted the spirit of his master's house (**53**).

SCENE 10: A LODGING-HOUSE
79 - 80
Difference: Encolpius does not return from the Forum but wakes in the night after Trimalchio's feast, finds himself alone in bed and sees Ascyltos and Giton sleeping together.

SCENE 11: AN ART GALLERY
83 - 87, **89 - 90**

SCENE 12: A BATHHOUSE
91

SCENE 13: A LODGING-HOUSE
92 - 99
Differences: the sequence of arrivals is different in the play and several events and details have been omitted.

SCENE 14:LICHAS' SHIP
100 - 110, **114 -** part of **115**
Many details of events on board ship have been omitted. Some

of Ascyltos' dialogue was originally Encolpius' or Giton's.

SCENE 15: A BEACH

part of **115**

The story of the widow and the soldier is told by Eumolpus on the ship (**111 - 113**).

The story of the cannibal creditors (**141**) appears near the end of Federico Fellini's 1969 film.

SCENE 16: CROTON

126 - 140

A long scene in the original. Differences from the play include:

* there is no argument between Encolpius and Giton;
* Eumolpus and other characters appear;
* Encolpius' failed love-making with Circe and his subsequent beating do not take place in a temple;
* Satyrion is not mentioned in this scene but as part of an orgy with Quartilla (**20, 21** - not included in the play).

SCENE 17: A LODGING HOUSE

The scene between Encolpius and Giton is invented. In **140** Encolpius watches through a hole in a wall as Eumolpus, with some assistance, and a girl have sex. Later Eumolpus, not Giton, is witness to Encolpius' recovery.

SCENE 18: THE LAST SUPPER

"Detained and unwilling to face fear or hope, Petronius did not hurry to take his life but caused his severed arteries to be bound up as he conversed with friends and listened as they rehearsed light songs and frivolous verses. He took his place at dinner and drowsed so that his death should at least resemble nature. In his will he did not follow the custom of flattering Nero but detailed the Emperor's debauches and each act of his lust."

(adapted from the historian Tacitus)